U.S. Intelligence

THE WASHINGTON PAPERS

. . . intended to meet the need for an authoritative, yet prompt, public appraisal of the major developments in world affairs.

MANUSCRIPT SUBMISSION

The Washington Papers and Praeger Publishers welcome inquiries concerning manuscript submissions. Please include with your inquiry a curriculum vitae, synopsis, table of contents, and estimated manuscript length. Manuscript length must fall between 120 and 200 double-spaced typed pages. All submissions will be peer reviewed. Submissions to *The Washington Papers* should be sent to *The Washington Papers*; The Center for Strategic and International Studies; 1800 K Street NW; Suite 400; Washington, DC 20006. Book proposals should be sent to Praeger Publishers; 90 Post Road West; P.O. Box 5007; Westport, CT 06881-5007.

The Washington Papers/157

U.S. Intelligence

Evolution and Anatomy

Second Edition

Mark M. Lowenthal

Foreword by David Kahn

Published with the Center for
Strategic and International Studies
Washington, D.C.

PRAEGER

Westport, Connecticut
London

Library of Congress Cataloging-in-Publication Data

Lowenthal, Mark M.
U.S. intelligence : evolution and anatomy / Mark M. Lowenthal. – 2nd ed.
p. cm. – (The Washington papers ; 157)
"Published with the Center for Strategic and International Studies, Washington, D.C."
Includes bibliographical references and index.
ISBN 0-275-94435-2. – ISBN 0-275-94434-4 (pbk.)
1. Intelligence service – United States – History – 20th century.
I. Center for Strategic and International Studies. II. Title. III. Series.
UB251.U5L68 1992
327.1′273′00904 – dc20 92-15913

The *Washington Papers* are written under the auspices of the Center for Strategic and International Studies (CSIS) and published with CSIS by Praeger Publishers. The views expressed in these papers are those of the authors and not necessarily those of the Center.

British Library Cataloging-in-Publication data is available.

Library of Congress Catalog Card Number: 92-15913
ISBN: 0-275-94435-2 (cloth)
0-275-94434-4 (paper)

First published in 1992

Praeger Publishers, 88 Post Road West, Westport, CT 06881
An imprint of Greenwood Publishing Group, Inc.

Printed in the United States of America

The paper used in this book complies with the Permanent Paper Standard issued by the National Information Standards Organization (Z39.48-1984).

10 9 8 7 6 5 4 3 2

Contents

Foreword

In the past three decades, intelligence has become a frequent topic of public discourse. Scholars dissect its history and publish journals on it. Newspapers advise on how best to use—or not use—intelligence agencies. Television documentaries about spies are commonplace, and intelligence is certainly no longer the closely held secret of government it once was. Moreover, the Central Intelligence Agency is famous; probably more people recognize "CIA" than "IRS."

The end of the cold war has intensified this trend. It has raised the most fundamental question of all: Should the United States even have an intelligence establishment? Although only a few would urge its abolition, many wonder how big an organization it has to be in a world with no perceived threat to U.S. power. They also debate the functions it should perform: gathering information on terrorists or drug lords seems reasonable, but disseminating business intelligence may create more difficulties than the task is worth.

This continuing public interest in intelligence, together with the changes in the U.S. intelligence organization since the first edition of Mark Lowenthal's exemplary book was published in 1984, explains the need for and the value of this second edition. Intended, like the first, to improve public discourse on the subject, it extensively updates and, where necessary, expands the first edition's material without losing its value as a compendium.

The problem facing someone coming fresh to this subject is not, as it was several decades ago, a dearth of information; the problem is a plethora. Needed is a concise guide to the intelligence community, so that a journalist, an academic, or an interested layperson can more easily find his or her way about in the maze of agencies and understand what they do, how they relate to one another, and how they came to be what they are. Bibliographies cannot fill this lacuna, and nearly all the books and articles on intelligence have been either too specific or too general to do so.

Mark Lowenthal filled this gap admirably with the first edition of his enormously useful overview of U.S. intelligence, and this revision maintains that usefulness. Like its predecessor, it is short, so its parts can be surveyed easily. It is well organized, so the relationships can be readily determined. It is pithy, giving only the most needed information. It is selective, dealing with the important agencies but not burdening the text with the multitude of secondary intelligence bodies, whose impact on national decision making is minimal. And it is veracious, imparting a feeling that this is how the intelligence establishment really works.

These qualities stem from Lowenthal's knowledge, capabilities, and experience. His studies for the Congressional Research Service taught him the organization of the intelligence agencies and their intragovernmental links – fundamental to understanding how those agencies work. His experience as a deputy assistant secretary of state dealing with intelligence gave him insight into the practical operations of intelligence – though I sought in vain for some indiscretions or revelations of classified material. His background as a contemporary American historian ensures his putting intelligence into context, both historically and politically. Finally – and this is perhaps the rarest faculty of all among those who deal with intelligence – Lowenthal can write.

All this has produced an extraordinarily valuable contribution to a major area of government activity that is clearly of national interest. By helping people better understand intelligence, Mark Lowenthal brings this still often secret area into the public discussion that democracy requires.

David Kahn
Author of *The Codebreakers* and
Seizing the Enigma: The Race to Break the German U-boat Codes

June 1992

About the Author

Mark M. Lowenthal is the senior specialist in U.S. foreign policy at the Congressional Research Service (CRS) of the Library of Congress. From 1985 to 1989, he served in the State Department's Bureau of Intelligence and Research, first as director of the Office of Strategic Forces Analysis and then as deputy assistant secretary for functional analysis. Prior to that he was a specialist in national defense at CRS, focusing on intelligence and arms control issues, and also served as head of CRS's Defense/Arms Control and Europe/Middle East/Africa sections. Dr. Lowenthal has a Ph.D. in history from Harvard University. His publications include *Leadership and Indecision: American War Planning and Policy Process, 1937–1942*; a novel, *Crispan Magicker*; and numerous articles and congressional studies on national security issues. Dr. Lowenthal was the 1988 grand champion on the TV game show *Jeopardy!* and is coauthor of *Secrets of the Jeopardy! Champions.*

Summary

No major twentieth-century power has so short a history of national intelligence agencies or activities as does the United States, and few have been as public or as tumultuous. Even as this book was being completed early in 1992, a major debate opened over the future structure, size, and role of U.S. intelligence in the aftermath of the cold war.

This book is divided into two parts, which can be read separately or together. Part I is a history of the U.S. intelligence community, beginning with its limited twentieth-century antecedents and emphasizing its growth and development after 1947. Part II describes the organization and function of the major components of the community as they existed at the beginning of 1992.

The history of the intelligence community can be divided into three distinct periods. From its creation in 1947 until the revelations and investigations of 1974–1975, the modern intelligence community operated under fairly broad grants of authority based on trust. The active prosecution of the cold war shaped much of what the agencies did, either in terms of analysis or operations (covert actions as distinct from clandestine intelligence collection), these operations burgeoning far beyond most expectations. Although each administration probably felt let down at some point by either a mistaken analysis or flawed operation, the basic producer-consumer relationship worked to both sides' essential satisfaction. Oversight by Congress, however, was very limited, in part a preference of the overseers.

Revelations of abuses and illegalities in 1974–1975 ushered in a new era that lasted until 1991. A previously dormant Congress was galvanized to write new oversight provisions and also took on a greater role as a shaper and consumer of intelligence. The relationship between the branches remained (and remains) at issue, as the Iran-contra scandal and its prolonged aftermath indicated. Moreover, the intelligence community now found itself operating in a much more open milieu on a regular basis. This may have improved relations with Congress, but it probably opened new antagonisms vis-à-vis policymakers in the executive branch.

The third and present period began with the collapse of the Soviet Union's satellite empire in 1989. By 1991, the Soviet Union itself was gone. Having contributed to the victory of the West in the cold war, the intelligence community found its role and even its necessity questioned by virtue of the absence of its major target. Both the executive branch and Congress reopened fundamental questions about the structure and role of intelligence in the post–cold war world.

Within these three periods certain themes have recurred: the clash between the necessary secrecy and an ostensibly open government; the distinct pulls of analysis and operations and the friction between these two types of activities; the difficulty of managing a wide and disparate community whose components serve a variety of customers with different needs; and the constitutional "invitation to struggle" that exists between Congress and the president in all areas.

In discussing the structure of the community, part II emphasizes both internal organization and function and how each component fits into the larger entity called the intelligence community. There are three main groupings:

central coordination and management, intelligence agencies and components, and oversight.

For most of its history, the community has been organized along the lines of what might be termed "purposeful redundancy," driven by the concept of competitive analysis as the best means of arriving at what is actually happening or is likely to happen. Interestingly, even this guiding principle is being questioned in the post–cold war debate about size and cost.

If this book has any distinct point of view, it is twofold. First, a competent and challenged intelligence capability is an essential part of the U.S. national security structure, regardless of the status of external threats or events. Second, the major requirement of this structure is providing timely, objective, and pointed analysis to policymakers across a wide range of issues. Some practitioners will question this bias in favor of analysis at the expense of operations. Both are important, but operations are more isolated phenomena. The need for good analysis is constant.

I

The Evolution of U.S. Intelligence

Introduction

This book is an update and revision of a book I wrote in 1984. I had two primary purposes in mind when I undertook this revision. First, a great many things had happened in and to U.S. intelligence in the intervening years, chief among them the Iran-contra affair and its fallout, particularly the changes in congressional oversight; the collapse of, first, the Soviet Union's satellite empire and then of the Soviet Union itself and their effects on U.S. intelligence; and the Persian Gulf War. Second, from 1985 to 1989 I had the privilege of serving in the intelligence community in the State Department's Bureau of Intelligence and Research, first as director of the Office of Strategic Forces Analysis and then as deputy assistant secretary for functional analysis. This professional experience and exposure led me to rethink many of the views I had held about how the intelligence community functions and relates to policymakers – key themes for this book.

Certain observations and themes of my earlier edition remain pertinent. First, this study does not purport to be a complete history of the U.S. intelligence community. Any history based on unclassified sources, as this one is, cannot claim to be complete. Nor can a study of this length treat many issues in depth. For that reason, I have relied heavily on footnotes to lead interested readers to fuller treatments of specific issues or events. Rather, this is a somewhat brief description and analysis of certain organizations, trends, processes, and products that have shaped and dominated U.S. intelligence since 1940. The following issues remain central:

- the existence of secret intelligence agencies in a democracy, especially in a post–cold war world that many perceive to be less threatening
- the contribution that intelligence can and does make to the formulation of national security policy
- the nature of the relationship between intelligence producers and intelligence consumers
- the competition between current and long-range intelligence analysis
- the relationship between intelligence analysis and operations
- the ability of Congress to oversee intelligence activities effectively and the willingness of the executive to abide by oversight rules.

These issues are not new and are not likely ever to be resolved with any finality. They tend to surface somewhat randomly over and over again, depending on the nature of external events and internal policies and decisions. Nonetheless, they remain the major poles around which the multifaceted debate over intelligence tends to revolve. At the time of this writing, they are being reexamined with some vigor, as the United States tries to come to grips with the recent drumroll of international change and its implications for the future of U.S. intelligence.

The two sections of this volume can be read independently; indeed, they may appeal to different audiences. Part I analyzes the issues noted above and how they have shaped the intelligence community. Part II delineates the current structure of the community and focuses on current organizational and operational issues. Both sections remain interrelated parts of the larger story.

U.S. intelligence operates in a highly charged atmosphere politically and often emotionally. Practitioners, veterans, observers, and my colleagues will undoubtedly differ with some of the interpretations and views expressed here. All of these are the author's alone, not those of any government agency.

1

Antecedents of the Modern U.S. Intelligence Community

Prehistory

Of all the major twentieth-century powers, the United States has the weakest intelligence tradition. Because there was no serious permanent external threat to U.S. security during the first 140 years of the nation's history, the United States kept all national security preparations to a minimum.

The current intelligence apparatus began to take shape in 1947, although a few threads can be traced back to the early World War II period.[1] The dearth of previous experience had two profound and contradictory effects on U.S. intelligence as it has developed since 1940. First, because there was such a limited base to build on, there existed wide opportunities and choices of activity for the nascent intelligence effort. The absence of tradition, however, also meant that there were few guidelines for intelligence, which, in turn, often resulted in questionable working methods and types of activities and attitudes that unfortunately developed into standard intelligence agency procedure.

The first major demand during the twentieth century for improved U.S. intelligence came during World War I, and the government response was typical. Only some prodding by interested subordinates prompted the expansion of the minuscule army intelligence efforts into a Military Intelligence Division (MID), which flourished only for the duration of hostilities. The Office of Naval Intelligence (ONI) seems to have had higher prestige within its service, but also suffered from lack of interest during peacetime. Moreover, these two groups were narrowly focused, concentrating solely on military intelligence pertinent to their respective services. During this period there was no "national" intelligence, as it came to be called, nor was there any coordination with the State Department's political intelligence collection.

Response to World War II

During the interwar period, U.S. intelligence efforts returned to the earlier minimal levels. As Secretary of State Henry Stimson reportedly said after he closed down the State Department's code-breaking unit: "Gentlemen do not read each other's mail." Nonetheless, the military cryptanalytic group began code breaking in 1932, concentrating on Japanese diplomatic codes; the first decrypts came in September 1940 and were called PURPLE. Beyond this important beginning, intelligence efforts during this period relied largely on the work of military attachés and the usual political reports from embassies. Foreign intelligence before World War II, as General George C. Marshall once noted, was little more than what a military attaché could learn at dinner over the coffee cups. President Franklin D. Roosevelt relied on his own sources—either his overseas contacts (largely British) or returning American travelers—a result of his preference for private channels.

In intelligence, as in all other major national security functions, whatever coordination there was tended to be informal or of limited value. The Standing Liaison Committee, in which the secretaries of state, war, and the navy met, typified both attributes, affording little more than an exchange of information. The Joint Board, which served as the army-navy planning body, often had prolonged debates that resulted in watered-down compromises. No effort was made to coordinate intelligence until June 1939, when Roosevelt formed the Interdepartmental Intelligence Committee to coordinate the Federal Bureau of Investigation (FBI), MID, and ONI efforts. This, too, resulted in little more than an exchange of information.

By July 1941, Roosevelt recognized the need for a better intelligence organization and created the Office of the Coordinator of Information (COI). The COI was largely the brainchild of William J. Donovan, an attorney, a World War I hero, and a Republican. A close friend of Secretary of the Navy Frank Knox, Donovan had undertaken official tours of Europe in 1940 and the Balkans in 1941 to assess the wartime situation. Donovan returned convinced that the United States needed a central intelligence unit encompassing a range of activities – collection, analysis, operations – and organized largely along lines similar to that of British intelligence, with which he was familiar.[2]

Donovan campaigned hard for this idea and was rewarded with the position of coordinator of information. The presidential order authorized him to "collect and analyze all information and data, which may bear upon the national security. . . ." This was to be made available to the president or his designees, and the COI had the right, with the president's approval, to request data from other departments and agencies, although he was not to interfere with the duties and responsibilities of the president's regular military and naval advisers.

An ambitious man, Donovan undoubtedly got less than he wanted in the COI position, but it was a start. Donovan used his authority to "coordinate" all national security information to begin building a research and analysis branch, known as R&A. Donovan also started two significant traditions. First, he drew heavily on the academic community. Second, he established a seven-member Board of Analysts, the lineal ancestor of the later producers of National Intelligence Estimates (NIEs). In all that Donovan did, the British influence in organization and approach was significant.

The COI spent much of the remainder of 1941 defending the agency's turf and seeking to enlarge it at the expense of numerous other agencies with overlapping functions, a bureaucratic anarchy that Roosevelt favored as it left him in control. In retrospect, the COI was more important for what the organization became rather than for what it accomplished.

The United States finally entered the war as a result of the greatest intelligence failure in its history, the undetected Japanese attack on Pearl Harbor. Pearl Harbor was an intelligence failure on a number of levels: various threads of information that might have indicated an attack were not promptly coordinated; analyses tended to rationalize Japan's behavior in terms of how the United States would act in a similar situation, failing to take into account wholly different national views, needs, and values;[3] there were gross underestimates of Japanese capabilities; analysts were, in the words of Roberta Wohlstetter, unable to distinguish signals from noise; the dissemination of information throughout the government was flawed in the extreme; and, finally, local commanders, fed only partial or confusing information, made poor decisions.[4] But Pearl Harbor also had an important aftereffect: by highlighting starkly the numerous intelligence shortcomings, the nation's leaders knew such a disaster must never be repeated.

War is a great simplifier (at times an oversimplifier) of policy decisions and functions. Although the intricate details of allocating resources are more complex, the larger issues of friend and foe and the general kinds of tasks that need to be accomplished are simpler than in times of peace. Intelligence is urgently needed in war, but wartime is not necessarily the best period for an intelligence organization to develop.

The early months of U.S. involvement in World War II saw another intense round of bureaucratic infighting, as old and new agencies and groups struggled for domain. Donovan fought hard for what he saw as an imperiled COI. The bulk of Donovan's organization survived, retitled the Office of Strategic Services (OSS). OSS was placed under the jurisdiction of the also recently formed Joint Chiefs of Staff (JCS) by military order on June 13, 1942. As such, OSS was to "collect and analyze such strategic information" as the JCS required, and to "plan and operate such special services" as they directed. Donovan was named director.

The OSS operated under a number of handicaps. First, there was the continuing competition with other agencies and producers of intelligence, particularly the FBI and the army's G-2. Also, OSS did not control the increasingly important signal intelligence activities. Moreover, as part of the JCS organization, the OSS had to compete with the Joint Intelligence Committee (JIC), which had been created to fill the needs of the JCS. Nor were the members of the JCS ever convinced of the utility of subversion, propaganda, and resistance groups in the struggle against the Axis. The British had first stressed these methods in military talks with the United States in 1940 and 1941. But these methods were rejected by U.S. military planners as too indirect and indicative of Britain's limited military capability, in which Britain was making a virtue of necessity.[5] It was the British model, however, that was once again influential in the establishment of the OSS.[6] Indeed, most of the initial operational expertise came from British mentors.

The OSS was organized into eight branches. R&A continued to be responsible for producing studies and estimates. Another branch was responsible for training and assignment. The remaining six carried out clandestine collection, propaganda, subversion, sabotage, and paramilitary operations.

The overall contribution of the OSS to the Allied war effort was modest. Although R&A assembled an impressive array of talent and produced some excellent studies and analyses, the OSS was only one of seven major intelligence producers.[7] Furthermore, there were nearly a dozen joint intelligence groups with specific functions or areas of expertise, as well as less important efforts housed in other agencies or groups. There was little coordination of their efforts; competition was promoted rather than controlled or channeled toward specific results. The absence of any regular lines of reporting and disseminating information also minimized the OSS's role as an intelligence producer, especially one for the president and his top national security advisers. The postwar histories of OSS stressed the more glamorous operational aspects of its work, further undercutting an understanding of its role as an intelligence producer.[8] The major contribution of U.S. intelligence to the conduct of the war was the effect of MAGIC, the translations of decoded Japanese messages, on the naval battles in the Pacific. In other respects U.S. clandestine collection, especially in Europe, was of no great consequence (with the exception of ULTRA—solutions of intercepted German messages—which the British shared with the United States).

The Legacy of OSS

As uneven as its record might have been in terms of the war effort, the OSS was the creator of many traditions for U.S. intelligence. First, it was an important training ground for an entire generation of intelligence personnel, both analysts and operators. Second, it gave these people an esprit that they carried with them as they stayed on in intelligence. Third, it established the tradition of housing analysis and operations within the same organization, demonstrating in some of its own activities the underlying tension between these two aspects of intelligence. Fourth, the OSS's difficulties in establishing a clear role for itself, because it was placed under the JCS and was not *primus inter pares* as Donovan envisioned, all strengthened Donovan's belief that a peacetime successor agency responsible to the president must be established. Donovan began campaigning for this in 1944. In so doing he once again aroused the opposition of the military, which hoped to control any central intelligence unit by making it responsible to a committee composed of the secretaries of state, war, and the navy, rather than directly to the president.[9]

2

The National Security Apparatus

The Demise of the OSS

The OSS was one of the first victims of the rapid postwar demobilization. The Bureau of the Budget recommended a return to departmental rather than central intelligence, with an interdepartmental committee for coordination. On September 20, 1945, President Harry S Truman ordered the termination of OSS operations effective October 1, 1945. Some OSS components survived, albeit dispersed. R&A went to the State Department, where it was united with other units to form the Interim Research and Intelligence Service. Truman hoped that the State Department would "take the lead" in coordinating intelligence. The War Department took the Secret Intelligence Branch (clandestine collection) and X-2, the counterespionage branch, combining them into the Strategic Service Unit (SSU). All three surviving branches continued their previous activities.

Toward the end of the war, a long series of studies and debates began over the proper national security organization the U.S. government should have. With the return of peace, these debates resumed with vigor. Although many issues were at stake – such as policy coordination, defense unification, the future of the air force, and the role of intelligence – much of the debate brought up the collective inadequacies that had contributed to Pearl Harbor. It became clear during the often heated discussions that neither the military services nor the State Department were willing to abandon responsibility for intelligence collection or analysis to a central agency. Nor did they want such an agency to be directly responsible to the president.

The Eberstadt Study

Secretary of the Navy James Forrestal, at whose request the reorganization debate had been postponed until after the war, now took the lead.[10] In June 1945, Forrestal asked his friend and former business associate Ferdinand Eberstadt to study the issue of military unification. Eberstadt did not confine himself to this issue alone, but went on to examine all the national security policy issues then under debate.

Eberstadt, undoubtedly remembering Forrestal's own preference for centralization, made recommendations that clearly presaged the eventual overall national security apparatus in many respects.[11] He recommended three separate military departments (army, navy, and air force) and a National Security Council (NSC) to coordinate the civilian and military aspects of policy. Under the NSC, Eberstadt recommended the creation of a Central Intelligence Agency (CIA) "to coordinate national security intelligence" and thus help the NSC perform its coordinative role.

In retrospect, it seems likely that Eberstadt meant only for the CIA to coordinate – not become a central producer of analyses in its own right. There was no basis or past experience from which such an analytical role could have derived. Nothing in the OSS's analytical performance would have suggested such a function.[12] Nor were the military services prepared to yield their own intelligence collection programs to a new central agency. They were only willing to go as far as Eberstadt's proposal for a coordinating role for the new intelligence agency that continued to recognize the independent requirements of the other departments.

The Birth and Growth of the CIG

On January 22, 1946, President Truman issued a presidential directive establishing a National Intelligence Authority (NIA) composed of the secretaries of state, war, and the navy, and the president's personal representative, Fleet Admiral William D. Leahy. The NIA was assigned to plan, develop, and coordinate the intelligence effort. Under the NIA, there was a Central Intelligence Group (CIG), headed by a director of Central Intelligence (DCI), responsible for coordination, planning, evaluation, and dissemination of intelligence, as well as overt collection. There was also an Intelligence Advisory Board (IAB) to advise the DCI, consisting of the heads of the military and civilian intelligence agencies. This, in essence, was not far from the JCS plan offered in rebuttal to Donovan's 1944 proposal for a central agency.

The major weakness of the new CIG was that its funds and staff were largely provided by the other departments, which retained autonomous control over their own separate intelligence efforts. Thus, from the outset, the CIG, like the OSS before and the CIA later, faced determined opposition. The first DCI, Rear Admiral Sidney W. Souers, who had drafted the intelligence section of the Eberstadt report, only held office for four months, as he was eager to return to private life.[13]

Much of the early work of the CIG was little more than simple reporting through the publication of Daily and Weekly Bulletins containing little analysis – a limited role accepted to avoid conflict with the other departments, particularly the State Department. The CIG's real opportunity came as the intelligence effort at the State Department foundered. Despite the tenacious resistance of Special Assistant Alfred McCormack, who was in charge of the renamed Office of Research and Intelligence (ORI) at the State Department, the unit failed to engender wide support either within the NIA or from Secretary of State James Byrnes. Facing congressional resistance to ORI's budget, Byrnes acquiesced to the wishes of his desk officers and distributed the former R&A officers among the department's geographic offices, leaving a rump Office of Coordination and Liaison (OCL).

Lt. General Hoyt S. Vandenberg succeeded Souers as DCI and proved to be more aggressive, although he seems to have regarded his assignment as a stepping stone in his career goal of appointment as chief of staff of the air force. A nephew of the influential Senator Arthur Vandenberg, the new DCI did succeed in gaining some budget independence for the CIG for personnel and supplies. He also expanded its role to clandestine collection, a role that reverted to the CIG from the War Department, and independent research and analysis. Vandenberg argued that he was trying to fill in current gaps rather than usurp any department's functions, a continuing special concern of the State Department. Thus, the CIG's role changed from coordinating national intelligence to producing intelligence. The CIG expanded in size and scope, especially its new Office of Research and Evaluation (ORE). Under Vandenberg, the CIG produced its first national estimate, prepared at the request of the president, on Soviet intentions and capabilities.

The National Security Act

It became obvious, not only to Vandenberg but to some NIA members as well, that if the CIG were to expand its role, it would require greater independence, including budget authority and legislative status. At this point Vandenberg's initiative became intertwined with the organizational issues still under consideration: national security policy coordination and defense organization. Indeed, President Truman felt that the CIG proposals to create a legislated intelligence agency were less controversial than these other issues.[14]

Although several drafts were required for the intelligence sections of the bill, the major controversy during drafting was the question of whether the DCI would be a military officer, which the JCS evidently preferred, and the effect this appointment might have on his career. The remaining sections of the legislation as they pertained to intelligence followed Napoleon's maxim about constitutions – that they be short and vague.

The omnibus bill had three major sections: the creation of a coordinating body for national security policies, the National Security Council; the creation of a National Military Establishment with three separate services (army, navy, air force) under a secretary of defense and with a statutorily created JCS; and the creation of a Central Intelligence Agency under a DCI.

Because there was a consensus that an intelligence unit with a legislative basis was needed, most of Congress's questions about that section of the National Security Act centered on specific details. Among these were questions about coordination between the CIA and the military intelligence units; about the chances of a "Gestapo-like" organization developing with intrusive domestic activities; and about the provisions allowing a military officer to be DCI, which raised questions about likely civilian control of the agency and whether this provision did not, in effect, mandate a military officer for the post. There was also concern about the vagueness of the CIA's duties as outlined in the original draft legislation and about whether the CIA's operations should include collection as well as evaluation.[15] Few questions were raised about the powers to be given the new agency; the question was whether these powers should be spelled out.[16]

In response to a number of these criticisms, the bill was revised to specify the duties of the CIA, specifically forbidding domestic police or law enforcement powers. Proponents also argued that proper coordination could be achieved through the NSC, to which the CIA would be responsible. The NSC was to be a civilian body, and this fact, coupled with provisions forbidding a military officer who was also DCI to command military units, helped answer fears about a military appointee. Moreover, some proponents argued that for the sake of coordination and operations a military DCI would be a good idea, at least for this initial period.[17] On the question of collection versus evaluation, General Vandenberg played down the scope and covert nature of the collection role for the CIA, stating that most collection would be overt and that the CIA would not supplant the current primary collectors but would coordinate this collection to avoid wasteful duplication.

The duties of the new agency as stated in the National Security Act of 1947 were all listed under the general task of "coordinating the intelligence activities of the several Government departments and agencies. . . . " These duties included (1) advising the NSC on intelligence activities; (2) making recommendations to the NSC on coordinating intelligence activities; (3) correlating, evaluating, and disseminating intelligence, although not on an exclusive basis and with a specific prohibition on "police, subpena, law-enforcement powers, or internal security functions." Included was a specific injunction that the DCI was to "be responsible for protecting intelligence sources and methods from unauthorized disclosure";[18] (4) performing those intelligence functions that the NSC believed could best be performed centrally; and (5) performing "such other functions and duties related to intelligence" as directed by the NSC.

Two points in this list of duties bear further note. First, the CIA was intended to act as a central coordinator and evaluator of intelligence, but not a separate collector or new producer. Indeed, President Truman's dissatisfaction with what he saw as haphazard and uncoordinated intelligence appears to have been a major factor in prompting him to support the creation of the CIA.[19] Second, the fifth mandated duty, "such other functions and duties" as directed by the NSC, was a shadowy area whose wider implications probably were not clear. These two areas of uncertainty, coupled with the brief but important traditions already established under the OSS and the CIG, would have a significant effect on how the CIA evolved and operated.

The Early CIA: Operational and Analytical Diversions

Throughout 1947 another important debate on intelligence paralleled that taking place in Congress. Policymakers were alarmed by continuing poor relations with the Soviet Union—especially by the Communist gains that had been solidified in Eastern Europe and by the fear that there would also be Soviet expansion in other directions. In response, the U.S. government considered initiating psychological warfare operations. The main point at issue was not the propriety of such operations, which were generally agreed upon as part of an overall more active resistance to Soviet expansion, but the question of which department should control them. Although NSC members seemed to argue that the State Department was the proper agency, Secretary of State George Marshall objected, believing that exposure of such a role could embarrass and undercut overt foreign policy. This role then passed to the new CIA at the end of 1947, largely by default, owing to an already existent overseas infrastructure and the availability of former OSS personnel with the requisite expertise.[20] Increasing tensions with the Soviet Union (the coup in Czechoslovakia and the Berlin blockade) helped promote an expansion of covert activities in 1948. Under the pressure of the cold war, the CIA followed the pattern established by the OSS—a division into operations and analytical branches.[21]

The CIA's first diversion from the coordinating of intelligence was quickly followed by a second—its emergence as another independent producer of short-term intelligence rather than broader estimates. It should have been expected that the CIA would have difficulties coordinating intelligence, given continuing hostilities among the already existing agencies. This, coupled with the lack of bureaucratic clout of the third DCI, Rear Admiral Roscoe H. Hillenkoetter, and the continuing demand for products such as the Daily and Weekly Summaries (first issued by CIG), helped move the CIA into its role as a producer of current intelligence, to the detriment of its role as a producer of estimates.

The preference of decision makers for current intelligence is easy to understand, given the press of immediate events and the often ponderous nature of longer estimates. Nonetheless, this shift in CIA focus had not been anticipated, and it seriously altered the CIA's role and its relationship with other intelligence components.

These difficulties and shortcomings were highlighted in a January 1948 study commissioned by President Truman to evaluate the CIA's effort and its relationship with other agencies. Allen W. Dulles, Matthias F. Correa, and William H. Jackson were chosen to direct the study. Dulles and Jackson both had wartime intelligence experience; Correa had been a wartime assistant to then Secretary of the Navy Forrestal.

The study group reported to the NSC on January 1, 1949, finding that the CIA had certain administrative inadequacies and lacked overall policy guidance. The report also criticized the CIA's failure to take charge of the production of coordinated national estimates. Items that were not national intelligence per se were being produced at the expense of the broader, mandated estimates. The authors argued that the current trend, which emphasized secret operations rather than intelligence coordination, should be reversed, that the CIA would benefit from civilian leadership (it then had its third successive military DCI), and that military appointees to the position of DCI be required to resign their commissions.

On the basis of this critique, the report proposed a large-scale reorganization to end overlapping and the duplication of functions. In place of the existing offices, the report suggested four new divisions—Coordination, Estimates, Research and Reports, and Operations – and close contact between them and the DCI.[22]

Some of the faults outlined in the report were legacies of the operational methods of OSS and CIG, including the emphasis on covert operations (OSS) and the production of short-range intelligence products (CIG). In part, the problem of coordination also reflected the difficulty the new agency was having in asserting itself in a competitive field.

3

The Age of Smith and Dulles

The Smith Reforms and New Agencies

The surprise invasion of South Korea in June 1950 added force to the criticisms of the CIA then being made in both the executive branch and Congress. In October 1950, General Walter Bedell Smith became DCI. Smith had been chief of staff of the Allied forces in North Africa and the Mediterranean and chief of staff to General Dwight D. Eisenhower when he was supreme commander in Europe. Subsequently, Smith had served as ambassador to the Soviet Union. Unlike Hillenkoetter, Smith was an extremely forceful administrator.

Additional impetus for change also came from William Jackson, who was the new deputy DCI. Under Smith and Jackson, a number of reforms recommended in the Dulles-Correa-Jackson report were enacted. The reforms are usually referred to as the 1950 reorganization, although in fact it went on through 1953.

Smith created the Office of National Estimates (ONE), whose sole task was to produce coordinated national intelligence estimates. Initially, CIA research was to be limited to economic changes in the Soviet bloc and carried out by the new Office of Research and Reports (ORR), while political research was to be done by the State Department. The Office of Current Intelligence (OCI) was responsible for current intelligence summaries, although it eventually began to do independent political research as well. In 1952 the Directorate for Intelligence (DDI) was formed, with responsibility for producing finished intelligence; it included ONE and ORR. That same year the competing operational offices (Policy Coordination and Special Operations) were merged into the Directorate for Plans (DDP), later retitled the Directorate for Operations (DDO) in 1973.

Other intelligence units were also reorganized during this period. In the State Department, Secretary Marshall reversed the decentralization permitted by his predecessor Byrnes and ordered a reorganization that created two offices – one for production and coordination and the other for collection and dissemination. This reversal was another stage in an institutional controversy that continued until 1961, centering on whether intelligence in the State Department should be centralized and separate from the policy-making offices so as to retain objectivity or decentralized and at the service of the various geographic bureaus and thus more intimately involved in the policy process. For the moment, centralization was favored.

Another important change within the State Department was the effect of the 1954 panel chaired by Henry Wriston, convened in response to a poor public image and low morale within the department. The panel viewed the Foreign Service as isolated from mainstream America – an in-bred group with limited diversity that spent overly prolonged periods overseas. The proposed solution was an infusion of outside talent and longer domestic tours for foreign service officers (FSOs). Within the intelligence area at State, "Wristonization" left a dual personnel system of FSOs and Civil Service employees – a mixture of greater operational expertise (FSOs) and greater in-depth knowledge (Civil Service) that continues to this day.

Another pertinent development of this period was the creation in 1952 of the National Security Agency (NSA) by a then-secret presidential order to unify ongoing military cryptologic activities. NSA was intended as and continues to be an intelligence collector, not a producer of finished analyses.

ONE: National Estimates

ONE now became the focus of national estimates production, promoted by Smith and Jackson and directed by Professor William L. Langer of Harvard University, who had been in charge of OSS's Research and Evaluation during the war and of the State Department's intelligence functions for a short period after the war. Langer carried out Jackson's concept of a Board of National Estimates, made up of senior government officials, academicians, and intelligence officers, which eventually became responsible for the review and production of National Intelligence Estimates or NIEs. NIEs were to represent the collective views of the intelligence community on major foreign policy issues. To produce these, the board was in turn supported by the ONE staff, which did the actual drafting. As originally conceived, ONE was to draw on the resources of other departments for its research support. Given the difficulties inherent in such a procedure and the CIA's growth as an independent producer of intelligence, ONE came to rely increasingly on the CIA. This meant that, at least during their early stages, the NIEs were CIA products. An interesting twist had now evolved. The CIA had been created to act as a coordinator of intelligence and to produce national estimates. In fact, it was producing those estimates in their initial stages and only later submitting them to the other producers for review. The entire process had been reversed.

Two factors caused the CIA's shift from coordinator to producer not only in national estimates but across the range of shorter-term intelligence requirements—political, economic, scientific. First, there was a genuine intelligence vacuum, which the CIA came to fill. Neither the military intelligence units nor the State Department produced the type of material then being increasingly demanded by officials at various levels within the executive branch, especially under the pressure of the Korean War. Moreover, in those areas where other producers did function, such as economic intelligence, there were often so many producers that responsibility for coordination naturally fell to the CIA. This gave rise to the second factor, the natural tendency of most bureaucracies to expand and thus further justify their existence, especially under aggressive leadership. Vandenberg, in trying to preserve CIG during its tenuous early days, had first promoted this tendency; Smith furthered it.

During Smith's tenure as DCI, the basic forms of the CIA crystallized. There now existed within the agency two complementary but largely separate groups—operations and analysis. Within the intelligence community, the CIA had become an independent producer, often competing with other agencies on short-range products and dominating the NIE process. Even more so than Vandenberg, Smith was an aggressive DCI. Under his successor, Allen Dulles, the role of the CIA expanded along the paths already laid out.

DCI Dulles

Allen Dulles, though not the "father of the CIA," was largely responsible for its increased role and influence on national policy.[23] Unlike his predecessors, Dulles came to the post of DCI with previous intelligence experience. During World War II, he had served in the OSS in Switzerland, where he directed operations against Germany. In 1948 he had participated in the report to the NSC that formed the basis for Smith's reforms at CIA. In 1951 he became deputy DCI. Thus, Dulles's background and major intelligence interest was largely operational. But, upon moving up to DCI in 1953, he also had more access to high policy quarters than any previous DCI, mainly, of course, through his brother,

John Foster Dulles, the highly influential secretary of state in the new Eisenhower administration.

Dulles's mark as DCI can be seen most clearly in a number of operations, both successful (Iran, 1953; Costa Rica, 1953; Guatemala, 1954) and unsuccessful (Indonesia, 1958; Tibet, 1958; Cuba, 1960–1961). Each operation followed a familiar pattern – the removal, or attempted removal, of a government deemed inimical to U.S. interests and its replacement by one that was more friendly. Such operations also reflected the widening scope of the struggle with the Soviet Union to areas beyond Europe and northeast Asia.[24]

Dulles's influence on intelligence products was more distant. In the case of NIEs, he did not become involved until the final draft was ready for presentation to the NSC or the United States Intelligence Board (USIB), a body created in 1958 to coordinate and manage intelligence activities.[25] During this period there arose a problem with NIEs that has continued to the present: their questionable utility at the highest levels of policy-making. A survey conducted by ONE in 1955–1956 indicated that rather than being influential at the intended level, NIEs were more customarily used by subordinate staffs as background for briefing their superiors. This problem has persisted to the present day, suggesting that perhaps too much was, and continues to be, expected of NIEs and that their theoretical utility far exceeds their actual use.

A major reason for this problem was the often ponderous nature of NIEs and the questionable intellectual and bureaucratic process that achieved "consensus" views. Driven by the belief that an agreed judgment on contentious issues could (or should) be reached – an idea much in vogue in the social sciences of that period, the NIEs became arenas for debate between agencies over fine nuances of meaning, leading either to language that was hedged and thus less useful to policymakers or to footnotes of dissenting opinions, which were again sources of debate.[26]

This removal from policy also marked, with similar effect, other CIA intelligence products. A sort of "dead zone" came into existence between producers and consumers. The producers did not have a clear idea as to what best suited consumers' needs; consumers did not attempt to define their needs any better and tended to ignore products that did not meet their immediate needs.

One of the hallmarks of the Eisenhower administration's approach to intelligence, and to national security in general, was the proliferation of managerial boards, a reflection of the president's own preference for well-delineated, well-coordinated staff work. An advisory panel for intelligence had existed since the creation of the CIG in 1946. Initially, in 1946, it was the Intelligence Advisory Board or IAB, which served as an advisory group for the DCI and was composed of the heads of the various intelligence services. With the transition from the CIG to the CIA in 1947, the IAB was replaced by the Intelligence Advisory Committee (IAC), whose function was to help coordinate intelligence and to set intelligence requirements. The DCI served as chairman, although he did not have budgetary or administrative authority over the other intelligence components, which of course made it very difficult for him to carry out his community-wide functions.

Intelligence community coordination remained a problem under President Eisenhower, although it must be noted that this aspect of intelligence had little real interest for Allen Dulles. In 1956, in response to a recommendation from the second Hoover Commission, President Eisenhower created the President's Board of Consultants on Foreign Intelligence Activities (PBCFIA), a group of experienced private citizens tasked to review intelligence activities periodically.[27] Although it was only advisory, the board did note the imbalance in Dulles's attention to his duties, a finding that had no practical effect. To strengthen the DCI's intelligence community role, the board recommended the creation of a new managerial body, the United States Intelligence Board or USIB, which replaced the IAC in 1958 without, however, any noticeable increase in the authority of the DCI.

The Missile Gap and the Bay of Pigs

Two intelligence controversies, one analytical and one operational, marred Dulles's final years as DCI. The analytical issue was the famous "missile gap" controversy of the late 1950s, centering on the strategic nuclear balance between the United States and the Soviet Union. In the early 1950s, the startling Soviet achievements in developing atomic (1949) and hydrogen (1953) weapons had led to overly pessimistic intelligence projections of the growth of Soviet heavy bomber and intercontinental ballistic missile (ICBM) capabilities.[28] The successful launching of Sputnik in 1957 renewed these fears. In what became a partisan debate during the late 1950s and the 1960 presidential campaign, Democrats – Senator Stuart Symington (a former secretary of the air force) and presidential nominee Senator John F. Kennedy, among others – charged that the Eisenhower administration was concealing an unfavorable missile gap. President Eisenhower denied these charges, based in part on dramatic photographic evidence from U-2 flights[29] and perhaps from ONE analyses, although he could not reveal the source for his rebuttals to give them added credibility.

Subsequent analysis by the new Kennedy administration revealed that the strategic balance remained heavily in favor of the United States. Although this stilled the immediate controversy, the significance of the missile gap debate was far-reaching for future NIEs on the Soviet Union. The intelligence community was perceived as having overreacted to Soviet military growth. Intelligence producers now feared that future overestimates would again damage credibility. A perception also arose among consumers and in Congress that NIEs tended to overestimate in order to present a "worst case." Some critics saw this as a desire to inflate the Defense Department budget, even though the intelligence community would gain nothing from such an outcome and might even lose scarce budget dollars. Thus, there was a dual effect: producers toned down their estimates, and consumers tended to discount the estimates to some degree as well.

The missile gap debate owed much of its sharpness to an underlying belief that some ultimate "truth" in intelligence estimates was attainable and that once an estimate was issued it was undesirable, if not positively dangerous to the credibility of the authors, to reverse it.[30] Had a different attitude prevailed – one that accepted margins of error or ranges of uncertainty as a fact of estimation and that saw revisions as necessary when new information was available – much of this and future similar controversies might have been avoided.

The operational failure that ultimately drove Allen Dulles from office was the ill-fated Bay of Pigs invasion in April 1961, an operation that overlapped the Eisenhower and Kennedy administrations. This type of operation was not unprecedented (Dulles had referred to CIA actions in Guatemala in 1954 when explaining the new operation to President Kennedy), but the scale of the Bay of Pigs operation was larger as well as more dependent on overt U.S. military assistance, and its planning much less well conceived. Although Dulles stayed on as DCI until November 1961, the Bay of Pigs fiasco undermined both his position and the standing of the CIA (and the JCS) with the new president.[31]

4

Intelligence and an Activist Foreign Policy

The Kennedy administration took office professing a more activist foreign policy approach, with an organizational arrangement that envisaged a more direct role for the president. Eisenhower's very elaborate NSC structure was scrapped in favor of a more barebones approach. Critics charged that Kennedy's arrangement lacked form, direction, coordination, and control and that it emphasized current developments at the expense of planning. Although the role of the NSC was downgraded, the role of McGeorge Bundy, assistant to the president for national security affairs, was expanded so that this adviser would have a more active policy-making position. Kennedy also allowed the PBCFIA to resign at the outset of his term and made no move to replace its members until after the Cuban debacle. On May 4, 1961, fewer than three weeks after the failed invasion of Cuba, Kennedy established the President's Foreign Intelligence Advisory Board (PFIAB), which resumed the duties of the old board in evaluating U.S. intelligence activities and agencies.

INR and DIA

The advent of the Kennedy administration also brought changes to the intelligence activities of the State Department and the military. The intelligence efforts of the State Department had vacillated between direct involvement with and distance from policy-making. During the later Eisenhower years there had been an increased emphasis on current analysis—that is, policy-oriented research. But the main effort of the Bureau of Intelligence and Research (INR), which was reorganized in 1957 to integrate production and collection, was on the encyclopedic country background studies—the National Intelligence Surveys. In 1961, Roger Hilsman, an advocate of a close relationship between intelligence and policy-making, took charge of INR. Many within the organization felt that Hilsman's approach necessitated subjective analyses written with an eye to policy preferences, which they bitterly resented. Hilsman dropped the National Intelligence Surveys assignment, which many believed had become a bureaucratic monster of little value, along with its CIA subsidy. He then reduced the size of INR, a step he later tried unsuccessfully to reverse.[32] The changes implemented by Hilsman largely set the pattern for INR down to the present.

A milestone in the development of military intelligence was the creation of the Defense Intelligence Agency (DIA) in August 1961. A part of Secretary of Defense Robert S. McNamara's effort to reduce overlap and duplication in the Defense Department, as well as to overcome the parochialism of individual service estimates, the DIA took over many of the responsibilities of the three service intelligence groups and oversight of those that remained with the services. The DIA's functions included the preparation of defense intelligence estimates, participation for the Defense Department on NIEs, and control of defense intelligence requirements and resources. Although the creation of the DIA could have been interpreted narrowly, within the confines of McNamara's managerial concepts, the agency quickly surpassed that rather limited role and became another independent producer of intelligence and an often intense rival of the CIA.

DCI McCone

The advent of John McCone in November 1961 brought significant change. Self-confident and still ambitious after a long and successful career in both business and government, McCone was much more interested in the production of intelligence and the DCI's intelligence community responsibilities than in operations, a view that President Kennedy fostered in defining McCone's duties.[33] Meanwhile, however, the DCI's authority to carry out his role as the "government's principal foreign intelligence officer" (Kennedy's words) remained limited.

McCone vigorously addressed his intelligence community responsibilities and succeeded in working out a sharing of the increasingly important overhead reconnaissance programs with the secretary of defense, which enhanced the DCI's collection requirements role through the USIB. In 1963 he also established the National Intelligence Programs Evaluation (NIPE) office to review and evaluate community programs, their cost-effectiveness, and the effectiveness of the USIB in implementing priority national intelligence objectives. Although limited in its ability to carry out these tasks, the NIPE proved to be an important step in allowing the DCI to fill his wider role.

McCone also became more active in preparing NIEs before a final draft was produced. He questioned drafters closely about their assertions and, on occasion, ordered reconsideration of the conclusions when he believed the Board of National Estimates had erred.[34] The most famous instance of McCone's exercising this prerogative (as all NIEs go out over the signature of the DCI) was in the early stages of the Cuban missile crisis in 1962. McCone signed off on an estimate holding that such a provocative step as placing Soviet missiles in Cuba would be wholly out of character for Khrushchev and too risky. McCone, however, acting in his role as the president's chief intelligence adviser, subsequently questioned this conclusion and urged Kennedy to order reconnaissance.

If Cuba in 1961 had contributed to a serious decline in the standing of the CIA, Cuba in 1962 was a source of its salvation. Although the initial predictions by the Board of National Estimates were wrong, U-2 flights confirmed earlier reports by agents and revealed the Soviet buildup in time for the United States to act before the missiles became operational. This success was largely a technical one, depending again on U-2 overflights. As the Senate Preparedness Subcommittee noted in its May 1963 review of the intelligence community's performance, however, collection capabilities outran the analytical capabilities to evaluate this incoming information.[35] This lag between collection and evaluation would grow as technical collection systems, particularly satellites, made rapid advances over the next years.

McCone left office in 1965, having found that his position of influence had declined with the advent of Lyndon B. Johnson as president. President Johnson, who did not take the same active interest in intelligence that President Kennedy did and therefore saw the DCI less often, relied more heavily on the secretaries of state and defense – Dean Rusk and Robert McNamara – for foreign policy advice. McCone also ran afoul of Johnson over the growing U.S. role in Vietnam, in which the DCI objected to the president's limited incremental steps, preferring a more direct and forceful approach. President Johnson did not tolerate opinions that did not buttress his own preferences, and McCone resigned.

President Johnson's choice for DCI, Vice Admiral William Raborn, was unfortunate. A retired officer, Raborn had been very successful as manager of the Polaris submarine-launched missile program. He had little foreign policy and no intelligence background, however, and simply was not taken very seriously by his subordinates or, eventually, by the president himself. He left office in little over a year.

DCI Helms and Assistant for National Security Affairs Kissinger

President Johnson now chose Richard Helms as DCI. Helms had spent his entire career in intelligence, beginning with the OSS in 1942, and thus was the first career intelligence officer to become the DCI.[36] Except for his tenure as deputy DCI under Raborn, however, Helms's entire career had been in operations. As such, he had less interest in the analytical side of the CIA and was aware that he lacked the detailed knowledge that analysts often had on some topics. Thus, Helms would remove himself from the initial drafting stages of some NIEs (although he followed some, such as the annual Soviet estimate, during interagency coordination), preferring to intervene during the final discussions at the USIB. Even here his contributions were more managerial in nature than substantive.[37] Helms appreciated that many of the issues at stake were ultimately unanswerable with a firm "yes" or "no," which seems to have contributed to a certain sense of detachment about the significance of the issues themselves.

Helms served as DCI longer than anyone except Allen Dulles, and for most of his six years, Vietnam remained the predominant policy issue, one that involved not only the CIA but all other intelligence producers and consumers. In a war fought with incremental measures rather than a more direct strategic plan, intelligence assumed a very different role. It no longer served merely to provide assessments of the enemy and estimates of operational success; it often became a political football as various consumers and others involved sought to support their positions. Acrimonious debates went on between military and civilian intelligence producers over various assessments, including one particularly prolonged debate over enemy strength.[38] In a war that had been overly quantified, intelligence was unable to retain its distance from those pressures that stemmed from policy preferences.

The intelligence community experienced a different pressure when Richard M. Nixon became president in 1969. President Nixon distrusted the CIA, as he did most of the bureaucracy, and thought that the missile gap controversy had cost him the 1960 election. Furthermore, Nixon intended to keep greater control over national security policy within the White House, working through the NSC.

President Johnson, like President Kennedy before him, had had a minimal NSC structure and relied more heavily on Senior Interdepartmental Groups (SIGs) for coordination. President Nixon, perhaps reflecting his years in the Eisenhower administration, reinstituted a large and formal NSC structure, relying heavily on his assistant for national security affairs, Henry A. Kissinger. The NSC structure eventually included the Intelligence Committee to provide guidance for national intelligence needs and continuing evaluations of intelligence products; the "40" Committee, responsible for covert action; and the Intelligence Resources Advisory Committee (IRAC) to "advise the DCI on the preparation of a consolidated intelligence program budget."[39] Kissinger chaired the first two committees. The DCI chaired the third, which was the successor of the 1968 National Intelligence Resources Board, itself an outgrowth of the budgetary work done by McCone's NIPE.

Under Kissinger the NSC went from a role of minimal policy coordination to one heavily involved in policy-making, advocacy, and intelligence assessments. Kissinger, rather than the president, became the main White House contact for the DCI, which made Kissinger, in the words of one analyst, "Nixon's senior intelligence advisor."[40] At the same time, efforts were made to improve the quality of intelligence, largely following the by now familiar pattern of enhancing the DCI's intelligence community role. The creation of the IRAC in 1971 was one part of this effort, although again real authority still escaped the DCI. One innovation introduced by Helms was the creation of the Intelligence Community Staff (ICS) in 1972 to support him in his community-wide role. Helms staffed the ICS with CIA employees, which limited their intelligence community role.

Although Vietnam remained the dominant foreign policy issue during the early years of the Nixon administration, it faded as U.S. direct involvement decreased. During this period the intelligence community became embroiled in more Vietnam-related controversies, including the situation in Cambodia before the U.S. incursion and the amount of supplies going to North Vietnamese forces through the port of Sihanoukville.[41] As the U.S. role in Vietnam declined between 1969 and 1973 (the year combat operations ended), more attention turned to strategic forces with the beginning of the Strategic Arms Limitation Talks (SALT) process and then to the various Watergate crimes, wherein President Nixon tried to use the CIA to block the Justice Department investigation.

Helms left the post of DCI in 1973, having been named ambassador to Iran. He was replaced by James R. Schlesinger, who had gone from the RAND Corporation to the Office of Management and Budget (OMB), where he had directed *A Review of the Intelligence Community* in 1970–1971. This study had resulted in renewed efforts to enhance the DCI's intelligence community role.

The Schlesinger and Colby Reforms

Although Schlesinger served as DCI for only six months, the shortest term since Souers's in 1946, his direction had a marked effect on the intelligence community. Believing that the DCI should play a strong and central role and that intelligence had to be improved, Schlesinger reduced the size of the newly renamed Directorate for Operations or DDO—the former DDP—and also made reductions in the analytic staff. To improve the functioning of the ICS, he introduced non-CIA employees. He became actively and substantively involved in the drafting of NIEs, especially those on the strategic balance, where he had a real understanding of the subject matter.[42] Observers agree that, had he stayed at the CIA, Schlesinger would have had a telling effect on the entire intelligence process, although many in the CIA were uncertain what the effect would be. In a series of reshuffles connected with Watergate, however, President Nixon named Schlesinger to be secretary of defense in the spring of 1973.

William Colby succeeded Schlesinger. Like Helms, Colby was a professional intelligence officer who had begun his career with OSS and, like Helms, had spent virtually all of his career in operations. Before his appointment as DCI, however, Colby was executive director of the CIA under Schlesinger; as DCI, he continued many of his predecessor's initiatives. The most important and controversial of these was the abolition of the Board of National Estimates and ONE and their replacement with a system of National Intelligence Officers (NIOs).

Colby believed that the board and ONE had become too insulated and inbred; appointment to the board was neither so much a recognition of ability nor as open to outsiders as originally but rather a fitting climax to a long career in ONE.[43] Continued consumer dissatisfaction with intelligence products also reflected the fact that the board was now quite distant from policymakers and thus not responsive to their needs.

Under the new system there were ultimately 13 NIOs, each with a functional or regional specialty and responsible to the DCI for intelligence collection and production within their areas of expertise. Although they served to coordinate the NIEs, the NIOs did not review the estimates collectively as the board had done, a process that Colby believed had glossed over differences and diluted final judgments. Defenders of the old system, and there were many, argued that although the NIO process would put intelligence producers in closer touch with consumers and perhaps sharpen the

NIEs, it also tended to narrow the focus by denying cross-functional review. These critics also claimed that the new system ran a greater risk of being susceptible to political pressure to produce specific analytical outcomes.

Colby assumed a managerial role in the NIE process that was more active than Helms but not as deeply involved in substance as Schlesinger.[44] He also introduced Management by Objective into the DDO process, to tie projects to specific program objectives, and Key Intelligence Questions, to identify intelligence needs better and then establish collection and production requirements. This innovation suffered, owing to the DCI's lack of authority within the intelligence community.

Although it may not have been apparent at the time, 1961 to 1974 was a tumultuous period for U.S. intelligence. It began with major analytical and operational setbacks and ended with a series of rapid changes of DCI for reasons largely related to an extraneous issue—Watergate. The underlying *leitmotif* of the period, however, was the degree to which the role played by the DCI, and hence the community as a whole, was so dependent on the wishes and demands of each president. Although the DCI's role as the president's intelligence adviser was exactly that envisaged by many framers of the National Security Act, few had probably thought about what this proximity cost. Nor was it apparent that changes in national attitude might later require the intelligence community to explain many of its operations and even analyses to the public.

5

The Great Intelligence Investigation

Disclosures

Much of Colby's tenure as DCI was taken up with the investigation of CIA wrongdoing, which eventually included all aspects of the intelligence community and its operations. In brief, the first allegations arose in relationship to Watergate, which involved some former CIA employees and an effort by President Nixon to use the CIA connection as a way of blocking the subsequent investigation. Then, in September 1974, the press reported that the CIA had undertaken the "destabilization" of Salvador Allende's Marxist government in Chile, which had been overthrown by the Chilean military in 1973.

Most sensational, perhaps, was the article by Seymour Hersh in the *New York Times* on December 22, 1974, alleging that the CIA had violated its statutory charter by undertaking domestic surveillance against U.S. citizens opposed to the Vietnam War and others, going as far back as the 1950s.[45] President Gerald Ford, who had been in office just over four months, immediately requested a report from Colby on these charges. Colby based his report on an internal CIA report on all past or present illegal activities first initiated by Schlesinger in response to the original Watergate-related charges, a report referred to at the CIA as the "Family Jewels."[46]

Executive and Congressional Investigations

After reviewing Colby's report, President Ford established a panel chaired by Vice President Nelson Rockefeller to investigate CIA activities "conducted within the United States." Internal and external pressure also grew for Congress to become involved in these investigations. Congressional oversight of intelligence had been largely limited to the Appropriations and Armed Services committees of both houses since 1947. Within these committees, oversight on certain issues such as covert action had been limited, a situation that dovetailed with a congressional preference to remain uninformed about certain intelligence-related matters.

A significant change in congressional oversight had occurred in 1974 when, in reaction to the Chilean revelations, Congress enacted the so-called Hughes-Ryan amendment. This amendment required that before expending funds for CIA operations in foreign countries (other than funds for intelligence collection), the president had to "find" that such an operation was "important to the national security" and report this finding "in a timely fashion" to the appropriate committees of Congress, including the House Foreign Affairs and Senate Foreign Relations committees. The Hughes-Ryan amendment expanded congressional oversight of covert action, although not necessarily on a prior basis, given the "timely fashion" provision.[47]

Both Houses now created select committees to investigate the new allegations, not necessarily restricted to the CIA. The Senate created the Select Committee to Study Government Operations with Respect to Intelligence Activities, chaired by Senator Frank Church, which was composed of six Democrats and five Republicans. The House created the Select Committee on Intelligence, chaired by

Representative Lucien Nedzi and composed of seven Democrats and three Republicans. Nedzi's role was seriously undermined following revelations that he had known about some improper CIA activities in 1973 as chairman of the House Armed Services Committee's Intelligence Subcommittee. After a month of controversy, the House abolished its select committee and replaced it with a new one under the same name, chaired by Representative Otis Pike and composed of nine Democrats and four Republicans. Nedzi was not on the new committee, nor was Representative Michael Harrington, who had released classified transcripts on CIA activities in Chile.

In June 1975, as these congressional investigations were getting under way, the Rockefeller Commission submitted its report. This report substantiated allegations of illegal CIA activities, including domestic spying and surveillance. It found that there were statutory ambiguities regarding the permissible limits of CIA activities within the United States in pursuit of the agency's authorized mission; that new congressional and executive oversight mechanisms were necessary, both for control and for the restoration of public confidence; and that the DCI bore too heavy a burden with both an intelligence community role and the demands of running the CIA. Many of the commission's recommendations were related to specific abuses. Other suggestions were similar to those that had been made earlier to relieve the DCI of much of his CIA-related administrative responsibilities to enable him to concentrate on his intelligence community position. The commission also called for a Joint Oversight Committee in Congress.[48]

Congressional investigations continued throughout 1975, dominating the news for prolonged periods and putting tremendous pressure on relations between Congress and the executive branch. Colby adopted the attitude that to complete the investigation, make a clean break with the past, and restore public confidence, it was best to be as cooperative as possible. This stance alienated Henry Kissinger, now both national security adviser and secretary of state, who thought Colby too cooperative. It also antagonized many of Colby's current and former colleagues in the intelligence community.[49] The executive branch had particular problems with demands by the House committee for intelligence documents, and at one point the committee filed a contempt citation against Kissinger for his refusal to supply State Department memoranda on the Turkish invasion of Cyprus and other issues. After a compromise was achieved, the citation was dropped.

The Church and Pike committees, as they came to be called, covered wide and divergent areas in their investigations. The Senate committee concentrated more on operations and questionable activities, including the CIA role in Chile, illegal mail openings, unauthorized storage of toxic agents, the role of the Internal Revenue Service and the FBI, illegal intercepts by the NSA, and covert action.[50] Among its more sensational areas of inquiry were assassination plots against foreign leaders. The committee found that active attempts were made against Fidel Castro and Patrice Lumumba and that U.S. officials either encouraged or were privy to plots against Rafael Trujillo, Ngo Dinh Diem, and Rene Schneider. It was noted, however, that "no foreign leaders were killed as a result of assassination plots initiated by officials of the United States."[51]

The House committee took a different approach, concentrating on the management and organization of the intelligence community and proceeding from there to assess how well the community had produced accurate and usable intelligence for decisions makers.

Before either committee issued its final report, President Ford reshuffled his national security advisers. On November 2, 1975, he dismissed Colby as DCI, replacing him with George Bush. This dismissal evidently resulted from the president's continued dissatisfaction over the way in which Colby responded to the investigations. At the same time, Schlesinger was dismissed as secretary of defense, owing to his disputes with Kissinger over strategic arms policy. Kissinger had to relinquish his post as assistant to the president for national security affairs and was replaced by his deputy, Lt. General Brent Scowcroft. Colby stayed on until Bush's confirmation; Bush took office in January 1976.

President Ford took further steps to reorganize the intelligence community on February 8, 1975, with Executive Order (E.O.) 11905, the first public directive on U.S. intelligence roles and responsibilities. This order once again reaffirmed the DCI's primacy in foreign intelligence and his intelligence community responsibilities and streamlined the number of groups controlling various aspects of intelligence. USIB, IRAC, the NSC Intelligence Committee, and the "40" Committee were all abolished. The USIB's functions were largely retained in the new National Foreign Intelligence Board (NFIB), created in May 1976; the DCI's management and resource control authority were handled through the new Committee on Foreign Intelligence (CFI), which reported to the NSC. President Ford's order also placed restrictions on certain activities and created an Intelligence Oversight Board (IOB) to monitor the conduct of intelligence components, largely via monthly reports of illegal acts or improprieties from the agencies directly to the IOB, bypassing the DCI. Although this executive order responded to some concerns raised by the investigations—including the DCI's authority, the increased role of the NSC, and executive oversight—it also raised a more fundamental question: was this the best method of reordering intelligence given the extreme mutability of executive orders?

The Pike Committee completed its final report first, but the House, after a heated debate, voted 246 to 124 on January 29, 1976, to withhold release pending a classification review by the executive, a reflection of a problem that had beset the committee. Pending that review, the committee released its recommendations on February 11, 1976, which included separating the DCI from the CIA to allow the DCI to concentrate on his intelligence community role, abolishing the DIA, and improving executive and congressional oversight.[52] The remainder of the final report became mired in controversy when sections of it were leaked to Daniel Schorr of CBS-TV, who in turn gave them to the *Village Voice*, a weekly New York City newspaper.

The excerpts from the draft House final report printed in the *Village Voice* on February 11, 1976, detailed numerous shortcomings in the intelligence community. These included what the committee considered loose budget procedures and controls, with limited accountability, and performance failures, including the Tet Offensive, the 1968 Soviet invasion of Czechoslovakia, the 1973 Yom Kippur War, the 1974 coup in Portugal, the 1974 Indian nuclear explosion, and the 1974 Greek coup in Cyprus. Overall, the report found that intelligence activities were not cost-effective and were unnecessarily risky, as well as illegal in certain instances. In its evaluation of U.S. verification of the SALT I agreement, the report found that the integrity of the intelligence process had been undermined by combining the evaluating and decision-making process in the person of Henry Kissinger.[53]

The unauthorized publication of the House report doomed any chance for official and full publication. Instead, the House turned its attention to the leak of the report to Schorr, which resulted in an inconclusive investigation by the House Committee on Standards of Official Conduct. Thus, the investigation of the House Select Committee on Intelligence ended on a note of contention and utmost disharmony.

At the same time, the Church Committee continued preparing its final report while the 94th Congress's Senate Resolution 400, establishing a standing Senate committee on intelligence, moved forward. The final report was released at the end of April 1976. The committee found an absence of necessary statutory guidelines, excessive use of covert action, a need for restructuring relations between the DCI and the intelligence agencies to improve management and oversight, and domestic intelligence activities that had violated specific statutory prohibitions and undermined constitutional rights. It recommended enacting legislative charters for all intelligence agencies; divesting the DCI of his managerial role over the CIA; enhancing the DCI's intelligence community authority over activities, programs, budgets, requirements, and resources; separating analysis from operations within the CIA; obtaining prior congressional consent for covert operations, thus indicating that the concept of such operations was still acceptable; improving oversight; and restricting the activities of intelligence agencies to prevent future violations of political rights and freedoms.[54] On May 19, 1976, in a fitting climax to the Church Committee's activities, the Senate voted, 77 to 22, to create a Select Committee on Intelligence to carry out these new oversight functions.

An Assessment

The 16 months between Hersh's articles and the Senate committee's report were a bruising period for U.S. intelligence. Morale and public confidence plummeted; the community itself was riven by deep internal fissures. Although there had been past disclosures of failures, such as the Bay of Pigs in 1961, or questionable activities, such as the 1967 revelations about CIA funding of the National Student Association, never before had the entire range of activities of the community been laid bare in so hostile an atmosphere. A clean break with the past now seemed unavoidable. U.S. intelligence would probably never again receive the carte blanche it had enjoyed. Moreover, intelligence products and activities would now be available to a much wider audience in the new Senate committee.

It is interesting to note the vast difference in the way in which the two investigating committees ended and the perceptions of their work that have survived. The Church Committee is generally given higher marks than the fractious Pike Committee, especially given the way in which the House committee's report was leaked and the petering out of the committee's activities. Indeed, much of the reputation of the Church Committee rests on the strength of its 2,685-page report, which included detailed discussions of the large range of intelligence activities, their origins, authorities, controversies, and a history of the CIA itself based on unpublished internal CIA histories. What was lost in this comparison was the nature of the two distinct inquiries themselves. The Senate committee's hearings focused on the more sensational topics such as assassination and use of toxic agents. The House committee methodically attempted to understand the basic functioning of the community and concentrated on what should have been, ultimately, the main issue – the quality of intelligence and its role in supporting policymakers. All this was virtually lost in the turmoil surrounding the leak to Schorr and thence the *Village Voice*.[55]

To a certain degree, both committees were products of their time and were the result of revelations about intelligence that followed too quickly after the loss of confidence in government engendered by the Vietnam War and Watergate. To many, these revelations only confirmed the view that all of government seemed out of control. This view has since been tempered by renewed recognition of the need for timely and accurate intelligence and recognition that some genuine damage was done to U.S. intelligence as a result of these investigations and the sensational atmosphere surrounding them. As events were to prove some 10 years later, however, intelligence would always be liable, regardless of the changes in oversight or management, to such operational problems and such sensational public probes.

6

Politicized Intelligence

After the investigations of 1975–1976, the intelligence community probably would have liked nothing better than to be allowed to get back to work and retreat from all the unaccustomed publicity. But confidence in the functioning of the community had been so shaken that both overseers and overseen had to demonstrate that the new controls were working and any retreat was probably precluded. Instead, much that the community did remained in the public eye, making intelligence much more susceptible to the push and pull of politics from which it had long been exempt.

Team A–Team B

After a relatively quiet summer and autumn, intelligence, specifically analysis, returned to the news at the end of 1976. Several newspapers reported as early as October 20 that PFIAB had commissioned a group of outside experts to review the NIEs on the Soviet Union, and these experts had found that the NIEs had underestimated the threat. Thus began the controversy known as Team A–Team B.

As the Senate Select Committee on Intelligence later reported, PFIAB members had been concerned about

NIEs' underestimating the Soviet weapons buildup as early as August 1975 and had suggested a competitive analysis at that time. Indeed, the NIE on the Soviet Union had always been a subject of controversy ever since the missile gap debate of the late 1950s. The NIEs were significant not only because of their assessment of the potential threat to the United States, but also because they had become a major means of justifying defense policy preferences within successive administrations.

Thus, Secretary of Defense McNamara took a jaundiced view of the estimation of the Soviet defense program after the ICBM overestimates in the missile gap were revealed. He was particularly wary of air force estimates, which he considered self-serving, a view later shared by Secretary Schlesinger.[56] Although the agreed numbers of Soviet ICBMs continued to increase, McNamara was able to explain this calmly, often by mirror imaging and assuming that Soviet goals and strategies reflected our own.

Nor was NcNamara the only official to question the NIEs for political reasons. As the Church Committee reported, in 1969 DCI Helms became embroiled in a dispute with Kissinger and Secretary of Defense Melvin Laird over whether the Soviet SS-9 ICBM had a multiple independently targetable reentry vehicle (MIRV) capability as opposed to a multiple reentry vehicle (MRV) capability (one in which the warheads were not independently targeted) and whether the Soviets sought a first-strike capability. These issues were crucial to policy decisions on MIRVing U.S. missiles, on SALT negotiation tactics, and on deploying antiballistic missiles (ABMs). Kissinger and his staff believed the SS-9 had been MIRVed and tried to get the Board of National Estimates to agree, which it did not. Laird objected to doubts raised over Soviet first-strike goals, as this contradicted his own public position. Helms agreed to delete the offending paragraph from the NIE, although the State Department reinserted it as a footnote.[57]

Therefore, PFIAB's concerns in 1975 represented part of a long process of questioning NIEs on the Soviet Union.

After examining an NIE at the suggestion of DCI Colby in 1975, PFIAB recommended a competitive analysis in April 1976, to which new DCI Bush agreed. Team A consisted of the intelligence community analysts; Team B consisted of three outside groups, chaired by Professor Richard Pipes of Harvard University, a Russian historian. Both teams were given the same data and asked to see if the data would support differing views of Soviet capabilities and objectives. Ultimately, Team B did arrive at a very different conclusion, denying the validity of the "mirror-image" assumptions and arguing that the Soviet goal was military superiority. When reports of the differences leaked, critics pointed out that Team B was composed of so-called hawks or alarmists – those with an initial skepticism about past estimates – and that its estimate was based on a "worst case" view.

Several issues were all but lost in the controversy, which resulted in an investigation and report by the Senate Intelligence Committee. Judgments in past NIEs had been questionable, although this might have been less of a problem had there not been a continuing perception that making radical changes from one year to the next would incur penalties in terms of credibility.[58] The utility of NIEs as a whole was questionable, given their size, the production time required, and the limited absorptive capacity of consumers. This issue, however, was not addressed at this time. Competitive analyses, as the Senate committee noted, were a legitimate exercise, although the Team B episode may have complicated such efforts for the immediate future. The Senate committee called for a reversal of the NIO system back to a "collegial estimative group."[59]

Jimmy Carter and U.S. Intelligence

Team A–Team B overlapped the transition period between the administrations of Gerald Ford and Jimmy Carter. DCI Bush, who had performed creditably despite doubts expressed over his "political" appointment, announced that he would resign at the end of the Ford administration, leaving Carter free to appoint his own DCI, the fifth in less than four years. Bush was willing to stay on to give the CIA some stability and to avoid politicizing the selection of the DCI, but his tenure did not fit in with Carter's plans for intelligence. Instead, President-elect Carter chose Theodore Sorensen, former special counsel to President Kennedy. As confirmation hearings neared, doubts arose over the Sorensen nomination, stemming not only from Sorensen's statements in favor of publicizing the CIA budget and limiting covert action, but also from his past behavior. The main issue was his use of classified material in preparing his memoirs and his affidavit filed in support of Daniel Ellsberg in the 1972 Pentagon Papers case that noted Sorensen's use of this material. His draft status as conscientious objector was also raised. By the time the Senate Intelligence Committee convened on January 17, 1977, for the confirmation hearings, a number of senators had already expressed serious reservations about Sorensen's appointment. In the face of likely rejection, Sorensen read a statement responding to the various questions raised and then withdrew his nomination. Three weeks later President Carter nominated Admiral Stansfield Turner, commander in chief of Allied Forces in Southern Europe, to be DCI. Turner experienced no difficulties with his nomination and was unanimously confirmed by the Senate.

The Carter administration had taken office with an attitude toward U.S. intelligence ranging from skeptical to hostile. During the election campaign Carter had referred to the intelligence revelations on occasion, sometimes grouping them with other scandals, and promised to be more careful in his use of covert action as a foreign policy tool.[60] Vice President Walter Mondale had been a member of the Church Committee; David Aaron, who had been on Mondale's staff on the committee, was now deputy assistant for national security affairs. This exposure contributed, at least initially, to a certain perception of the role of intelligence in policy and the ultimate use of intelligence made by the new administration. Concerns over Carter's attitude may have also affected the support that the intelligence community gave the president. The management of and use of intelligence, in any case, continued to be issues throughout President Carter's term, and a number of "intelligence failures" again preoccupied the executive branch, Congress, and the public.

Very early in his term President Carter was accused of using intelligence for political ends, when he cited the CIA report, "The International Energy Situation: Outlook to 1985," to buttress his call for a new energy policy. Some critics charged that this unilateral declassification politicized intelligence; others attacked the report's findings of growing shortages and price increases because these conclusions depended heavily on analysis showing that the Soviet Union would become a net importer of oil by the mid-1980s, a conclusion that some experts questioned. The Senate Intelligence Committee staff investigated the production and release of the CIA report and concluded that, although the integrity of the analytical process was intact, President Carter did have political motives in releasing the report. Although this was not improper, the manner in which he released the report was deemed questionable.[61] This was the second time in five months that intelligence analysis, not operations, had become a political issue.

Because of the unsettled state of the intelligence agencies after the investigations, President Carter moved to reshape and put his own stamp on them. He also faced a new situation: the existence of first one and then two strong oversight committees in Congress.

In May 1977 President Carter abolished PFIAB while retaining the Intelligence Oversight Board, claiming that the congressional committees made PFIAB redundant. This view was either a misunderstanding of PFIAB's role or merely an excuse. In fact, the PFIAB members were too conservative for President Carter. Like his predecessors, President Carter then moved to augment the DCI's intelligence community-wide authority over priorities, tasking, and budget, first in a reorganization in August 1977 and then through E.O. 12036, signed on January 24, 1978.

E.O. 12036 was the result of tripartite negotiations among the White House, the intelligence community, and the Congress. It again reaffirmed the role of the NSC, which President Carter had greatly scaled down, recognized the existence of the National Foreign Intelligence Board and the new but ultimately abortive National Intelligence Tasking Center, and specified the central role of the DCI, including his "full and exclusive authority" for the National Foreign Intelligence Program (NFIP) budget. The order also listed a number of restrictions on collection techniques, participation in domestic organizations, human experimentation, and a ban on assassinations—all reactions to the recent revelations. For the first time the intelligence functions of all intelligence agencies or groups (CIA, State, Defense, Treasury, Energy, DIA, FBI, Drug Enforcement Administration or DEA) were made public. The issuance of this executive order, the second one in less than two years, renewed questions about whether an executive order was a satisfactory method of administering intelligence, as opposed to permanent legislation, the first draft of which the Senate Intelligence Committee was then completing.

DCI Turner

DCI Turner also became the subject of controversy when he announced in August 1977 a planned reduction of some 800 positions in the DDO, to be carried out largely through attrition. Turner said that the directorate's headquarters staff had to be reduced, as had the staff in the field after Vietnam. He also hoped to open up higher ranks to more junior officers. On October 31, 1977, Turner fired 198 employees (later 212), an event that became known as the Halloween Massacre. Plans for the reduction of the DDO actually went back to Schlesinger, Colby, and Bush, but this did little to make the dismissals any more palatable or less controversial, especially because of the brusque way in which they were carried out.[62] Critics also charged that Turner was downgrading human intelligence in favor of technical collection systems, which could not obtain information about plans or intentions.[63] Over the next several weeks Turner continued reductions, removing at least eight station chiefs (those in charge of CIA operations abroad or posted in major U.S. cities) and Deputy Director for Operations William Wells, who had signed the original dismissals. These dismissals seriously affected morale at CIA, even among those officers for whom "room at the top" was being created, and hurt Turner's relationship with that agency. News reports in February 1979 that 200 middle- and senior-level managers were seeking early retirement to obtain their maximum benefits were seen by many as reflecting the low state of morale.

On the analytical side, Turner took an active role in the NIE process, assuming the full authority implicit in the concept of the NIE as the DCI's paper. Turner was involved throughout the drafting process, suggesting changes, choosing among major alternative views to be presented, and sometimes adding a dissent of his own.[64] Although these activities were clearly within the DCI's role, Turner's critics, of whom there were many, said that he made changes based on personal interpretations of policy preferences among consumers.

Congressional Oversight

The state of congressional oversight was uneven when the Carter administration took office. In the Senate there was a select committee that had been functioning for several months; no such committee existed in the House. One issue that the Senate committee addressed was releasing a public figure for the intelligence budget. Turner, speaking for the Carter administration, testified that the publication of an aggregate figure for the entire community was acceptable. Others, including representatives of the Association of Former Intelligence Officers (AFIO), a pro-intelligence group formed in 1975 in reaction to the investigations, argued that even an aggregate figure would be of immense help to hostile nations.[65] Ultimately, no aggregate figure was released, although the budget authorization for the Intelligence Community Staff was made public every year from 1977 until its dissolution in 1992. Moreover, the issue of releasing an aggregate budget figure resurfaced some 13 years later, in the aftermath of the cold war.

More significant was the publication of the Senate committee's first annual report on May 18, 1977.[66] The report found that the intelligence agencies were "now functioning under the control of the President, the DCI . . . and they are now fully and properly accountable to Congress." The committee also noted that its relationship with the agencies was good, despite some difficulties concerning clandestine collection and foreign agents in the United States, and that the committee had been informed of every covert action requiring a presidential finding prior to implementation and had formally voted on all covert action projects in the new authorization bill. The success of the committee in working out a relationship in an unknown and highly sensitive area was the result of some very hard work from which committee members derived little or no personal political benefit. Much of the credit deservedly went to the committee's chairman, Senator Daniel Inouye.

The Carter administration actively encouraged the House to establish a committee of its own, which it did in July 1977, creating the House Permanent Select Committee on Intelligence. Although the basic charter of the House committee was similar to that of the Senate's, there was one striking difference. The Senate committee was bipartisan – the majority having only one more member than the minority regardless of the composition of the Senate. House Republicans had tried in vain to achieve the same arrangement for their new committee, but the House Democratic leadership refused. The new committee's initial ratio was nine Democrats to four Republicans. Although the party ratio in the House committee did not seriously undermine its work over the next several years, neither did it engender the bipartisan spirit that seemed to typify the Senate committee.

The major effort facing both committees was the enactment of statutory charters for the intelligence community, to set into law the organization, the role, and the limits on U.S. intelligence activities. After a year of work, the Senate committee introduced a generally agreed upon draft, the National Intelligence Reform and Reorganization Act of 1978, popularly known by its number, S. 2525 (95th Congress).[67]

A massive 263-page bill, S. 2525 represented more a beginning point for hearings and discussions than a final legislative vehicle. Many of its ideas were controversial: separating the DCI (to be retitled the director of national intelligence) from the CIA, rigorous review and notification procedures for covert action and clandestine collection, numerous reporting requirements from intelligence agencies to Congress, and a long list of restricted or banned activities. Each of these raised criticism from numerous witnesses. Separating the DCI might deprive him of a strong institutional base and subject him to more pressure from policymakers. The reporting requirements were criticized as being so numerous as to surpass any possible utility for Congress. Many witnesses objected to the long list of banned activities, finding it imprecise or implicitly sanctioning those activities not listed and, in the words of Clark Clifford, offensive and meaningless. Although only intended as a talking paper, S. 2525 undoubtedly ran into more opposition than some of its drafters had expected. The measure was not reported out of the Senate Intelligence Committee.

The quality of intelligence became an ongoing, major area of emphasis for both congressional committees. In February 1978 the Senate committee issued its report on the Team A–Team B exercise. The House committee's first annual report, issued on October 14, 1978, found intelligence products generally responsive to policy consumers' needs, but noted shortcomings in "estimating, forecasting and trend analysis." The report also noted an overemphasis on improved collection at the expense of other needs, as well as problems in having consumers set forth their intelligence requirements.[68]

Questionable Intelligence: Iran

Despite efforts by the Carter administration to make analysis more relevant to consumer needs, intelligence production evidently did not improve sufficiently to meet President Carter's expectations. On November 11, 1978, he wrote a terse note to Turner, Secretary of State Cyrus Vance, and Assistant to the President for National Security Affairs Zbigniew Brzezinski, stating, in part, "I am not satisfied with the quality of political intelligence."[69]

The main issue prompting this complaint was Iran. A year after President Carter's note, the seizure of U.S. hostages at the embassy in Tehran transformed Iran into the dominant issue for the remainder of his term. In January 1979, the Subcommittee on Evaluation of the House Intelligence Committee issued a staff report on the intelligence community's performance on Iran up to November 1978. The report blamed both producers and consumers for the "failure" to assess properly the depth of Iranian discontent with the shah. Collection and field reporting were considered weak, with no contacts with the religious opposition because of U.S. policy not to make such contacts lest they offend the shah. Production was judged "no better than fair," with much harsh criticism leveled at the entire NIE process, which was seen as "inherently cumbersome and time-consuming" and certainly ill-suited to a fast-breaking situation. In a devastating critique the staff added: "The mechanics of NIE production tend to discourage a sound intellectual process," and "the NIE is not worth fighting for." The staff report also found that the intelligence "environment . . . lacks incentives for the analysts to challenge conventional wisdom."[70] Although prompted by the worsening situation in Iran, the House report had identified glaring weaknesses across a wide spectrum of intelligence activities, using some of the harshest words ever uttered publicly about U.S. intelligence analysis.

Some of the flaws that led to the initial intelligence lapse in Iran, such as poor contacts and policy preferences affecting intelligence collection and analysis, helped lead to the second lapse—the seizure of the U.S. embassy in November 1979.[71] Certainly there were sufficient signals that, in the aggregate, should have provided some warning at the time. The major one was the initial, brief seizure of the embassy on February 14, 1979. Even a cursory reading of Iran's domestic situation should have indicated the internal weakness of the Bazargan government, on which much reliance was placed. Trying to reach accommodation with a regime whose members the United States had previously ignored, the Carter administration chose to overlook the dangers in the hope that normal conditions might soon prevail and normal relations would resume. Indeed, encouraging such a course in the face of its inherent unreality was the main focus of U.S. policy in Iran during 1979. The prolonged hostage situation was the result.

SALT II

Events in Iran seriously affected another crucial issue—the verification of SALT II. Improvements in technical collection systems, beginning with the U-2 and then satellites of rapidly increasing sophistication, made possible tremendous gains in intelligence. In no area of national security was this more important than in strategic competition with the Soviet Union.[72]

National Technical Means (NTM), as the mostly space-borne intrusive systems came to be called in SALT I, actually made the SALT agreements possible. Both powers regularly used such systems to keep track of strategic developments before there was a SALT agreement. Without NTM, neither side could have entered into even the limited SALT I agreement with any sense of security. Indeed, the capabilities and limitations of NTM became a driving force in determining the shape of SALT I, focusing the agreement on deployed launchers, which could be monitored with certainty, rather than on actual weapons, which could not.

The handling of verification had been an area of major controversy for a considerable time.[73] The Pike Committee had faulted Henry Kissinger, in particular, for dominating the verification process, in which he had a vested interest because he was also the main architect of the SALT I agreement. The debate over possible Soviet violations of SALT was, at that time, largely an accuser's game, with the U.S. government believing it could not refute charges without revealing important information about NTM capabilities. Thus, instead of becoming a means of building confidence, verification became an issue of major contention, with critics charging numerous Soviet violations that the United States apparently countenanced.[74]

Some of the crucial U.S. monitoring was done from two locations in northern Iran called Tackman I and II. These sites were line-of-sight radar installations – that is, monitoring posts with a direct "view" of the Soviet test launch center at Tyuratam, some 600 miles away. Soon after the fall of the shah, the United States abandoned them.

The timing was critical, as the SALT II agreement was in its final stages of negotiation. Verification loomed as a major issue in the pending debate in the Senate, not only because of past verification controversies, but also because the new treaty would go from the purely quantitative limits of SALT I to include some qualitative restrictions as well. For these tasks, and for the overall acceptability of SALT II to the Senate, U.S. monitoring capabilities would be crucial.

From the beginning of 1979, administration spokesmen, including President Carter and Secretary of Defense Harold Brown, issued assurances minimizing the effect of the loss of the Iranian sites.[75] In secret testimony before the Senate Intelligence Committee on April 3, 1979, however, DCI Turner stated that the lost capabilities could not be fully replaced until 1984. Nine days later he created a furor by eschewing any role for himself or the CIA in assessing "verifiability," stating, correctly, that the DCI and the CIA were concerned with monitoring (intelligence collection) and not verification (policy decisions on compliance). Turner's secret testimony was leaked on April 16, 1979, prompting quick rebuttals by the State Department and Secretary of Defense Brown, both stressing the continuing capabilities to verify SALT II adequately.[76]

Another concern was the security of U.S. monitoring technology. One satellite, the KH-11, played a major role in this area. In 1978, William Kampiles, a former low-level CIA employee, sold a classified manual describing the KH-11 to the Soviet Union; he was convicted in November 1979 and sentenced to 40 years in prison. This was the second time U.S. reconnaissance satellites had been compromised in less than two years. In January 1977, Christopher Boyce, an employee of TRW in California, was arrested with a friend for selling CIA communications and code information to the Soviet Union. Many in the intelligence field considered these cases to be among the most damaging for the United States up to that time. Both raised disturbing questions about personnel and security procedures within the intelligence community, given the ease with which Boyce received clearance, the lax security in the TRW facility, and the number of KH-11 manuals that could not be accounted for, as revealed in the Kampiles trial.

Thus, by the time President Carter and Soviet President Leonid Brezhnev signed SALT II on June 18, 1979, verification was already a highly contentious issue. Three Senate committees – Armed Services, Foreign Relations, and Intelligence – considered SALT II. In the Senate Foreign Relations Committee, the major verification issue centered more on procedural methods to improve confidence between the signatories and improved congressional oversight of U.S. verification decisions than on possible areas of monitoring inadequacies.

On October 5, 1979, the Senate Intelligence Committee issued an unclassified version of its report on U.S. monitoring capabilities. Although the committee predicted vigorous Soviet exploitation of ambiguities, it also expressed general satisfaction with current U.S. monitoring capabilities. The committee found that SALT II enhanced monitoring of the systems subject to the treaty but, at the same time, warned against "arbitrary resource constraints" that would limit future capabilities, urging the intelligence community to study Soviet negotiating strategy and tactics for "warning signs" of future Soviet weapons developments. The committee also favored periodic future competitive analyses of these developments, once again endorsing the general concept first attempted in the Team A–Team B exercise.[77] The Senate Foreign Relations Committee, in its final report on SALT I, echoed some of these concerns, including the problem of inadequate redundancy in U.S. monitoring capabilities, the need for adequate funding, and the need for continuing review of U.S. capabilities.[78]

SALT II did not come up for a vote in the Senate; it was pushed aside by a number of issues in which other questions of intelligence were significant. Chronologically, the first issue was a reported Soviet combat brigade of 2,000 to 3,000 in Cuba. Reports of its presence surfaced at the end of August 1979, and the chairman of the Senate Foreign Relations Committee, Senator Frank Church, facing a tough 1980 reelection challenge from a conservative opponent, promptly suspended consideration of SALT II until the issue was clarified.

One of the first charges to surface regarding the Soviet brigade was that of a U.S. intelligence failure. The Carter administration readily admitted that surveillance of Cuba had declined beginning with President Carter's January

1977 decision to suspend flights of the SR-71 reconnaissance aircraft over the island as part of an effort to improve U.S.-Cuban relations. These monitoring flights were not resumed until November 1978, when additional evidence of Soviet activity began to accumulate. Another hiatus in the overflights followed, although further evidence was collected during the summer of 1979. This additional evidence led the National Foreign Assessment Center (NFAC), formerly the DDI, to conclude in August that the Soviet troop formation was a combat unit, not a training unit.[79] The flights were resumed in October 1979 after the whole issue had been made public.

Ultimately, the brief furor over the Soviet Brigade petered out following a speech by President Carter stating that the unit may have been in Cuba since the mid-1970s. In his speech, the president also said that intelligence efforts aimed at Cuba were being increased and then restated his support for SALT II. Serious harm had already been done to the treaty, however, which further events would now cripple.

It was widely thought that the Soviet brigade issue had been poorly handled, and the perceptions of failure were reinforced by two dramatic events in quick succession. On November 4, 1979, the U.S. embassy in Tehran was seized for the second time, with more than 70 people initially held hostage. The failure to anticipate and prepare for such a possibility, the second in less than nine months, also had serious implications for intelligence and its use. Finally, in December 1979, the Soviet Union invaded Afghanistan to prop up the regime of Babrak Karmal. This action brought U.S.-Soviet relations to a low point. On January 3, 1980, President Carter asked the Senate to defer floor debate on SALT II indefinitely.

Iran, the Soviet brigade, and SALT II all reinforced the politicization of intelligence that had been evident at least since the investigations in the mid-1970s. To a certain extent this was unavoidable in an open, democratic government. The postinvestigation atmosphere, however, probably exacerbated this tendency. In the best of times these issues would have been highly contentious. Coming when they did, after the investigations and just before a presidential election in which the conduct of foreign policy would be a major issue, made a difficult situation worse.

Congressional and Executive Reform

These various events gave renewed impetus to the issue of charter legislation for intelligence, which had been stalled in prolonged debate among Congress, the administration, and the intelligence community. In his State of the Union address on January 23, 1980, President Carter spoke of the need for such legislation and, while mentioning his concern over safeguarding constitutional rights, also said, "We need to remove unwarranted restraints on America's ability to collect intelligence." A new bill, S. 2284 in the Senate and H.R. 6658 in the House (96th Congress), was introduced in February 1980. Ironically, the events that made it possible to introduce these bills also seriously impeded any chance of their passage.

The new bill, now entitled the National Intelligence Act of 1980, was shorter than its predecessor, but still of considerable length (172 pages). Many of the more controversial sections of the original bill had been changed, including the large number of separate reporting requirements and the detailed list of restricted covert activities. Others remained, including the redesignation of the director of national intelligence, his possible separation from the CIA, and limits on permissible covers for intelligence agents. One new feature of the bill was the levying of criminal penalties for the disclosure of classified information identifying an undercover intelligence agent. Efforts to identify intelligence agents had been of growing concern. Richard Welch, the CIA station chief in Athens, had been so identified and was killed in December 1975. The subsequent activities of former CIA officer Philip Agee and of the U.S.-based publication

Covert Action Information Bulletin in publicizing the names of other CIA officers, often mistakenly, had outraged members of Congress.

Hearings on the bill opened in the Senate Intelligence Committee on February 21, 1980, beginning with DCI Turner. Although there were still recognized differences between Congress and the executive branch over certain matters, committee members believed these differences were minimal. Turner's testimony outlined at least eight objections to the legislation, and he stunned the senators when, in discussing the proposed requirement for prior notice of covert action, he mentioned that he had not always given notice in the past despite the understanding with Congress. In subsequent testimony Turner said his remarks had been misinterpreted by the press. Later press accounts stated that Turner had told the committee in private that he had misunderstood their question and so had answered inappropriately. All in all, the legislation got off to a rocky start, and the pressure of the upcoming election made passage of the National Intelligence Act improbable.

Major pressure had also been building to revise the Hughes-Ryan amendment, which made notification of covert action to eight congressional committees mandatory.[80] In theory, some 175 members of Congress should have been briefed, although in reality the number was much smaller. Many critics charged that Hughes-Ryan had severely curtailed foreign cooperation with U.S. intelligence agencies.

Efforts to revise Hughes-Ryan were introduced in separate legislation, reducing the reporting requirement to the two Intelligence committees. The Senate Intelligence Committee formally abandoned S. 2284, substituting new language that provided a statutory basis for congressional oversight of intelligence and revised Hughes-Ryan so that only the Intelligence committees would receive reports, normally in advance of any covert action.[81]

After an incredibly complex legislative tie-up, a compromise was reached, retaining the Senate's three-tiered notification system (prior notice, limited prior notice, or waiver) even though the House Intelligence Committee preferred not to allow a waiver. At the same time, the Senate accepted the House's language to foreclose the executive branch's withholding of information on the grounds of classification or protection of sources and methods. The final enactment of this bill was a significant achievement. Congress now had a statutory basis for intelligence oversight rather than a mere "understanding," Hughes-Ryan had been revised, and the reporting of covert action to Congress would customarily be on a prior basis. Yet, the charter legislation had been abandoned once again.

In January 1980 the NIE apparatus underwent its second reorganization with the announcement that the National Intelligence Council (NIC) had been created. The NIC was a hybrid organization, combining features of the Board of National Estimates and the NIO system. The number of NIOs was reduced from 13 to 8 (6 for regions, one each for strategic and general purpose forces). The NIO remained responsible for NIEs in his field. The NIC would review NIEs for quality, as had the board, relying on four new NIOs-at-large. The NIOs would also have small staffs of experienced analysts to aid in preparing reports and NIEs. This staff, it was hoped, would overcome the NIOs' difficulties in finding drafters for their estimates. The creation of the NIC was a recognition that the NIEs, in theory the premier intelligence community product, were not fulfilling expectations or needs.

Hearings by the House Foreign Affairs Committee early in 1980 buttressed this impression. In addition to finding problems in NIE utility and timeliness, the Subcommittee on International Security and Scientific Affairs also found that collection capabilities were outrunning analytic capabilities, that there were shortcomings in human intelligence capabilities, and that CIA morale had suffered. The findings also noted an important issue that had too often been lost in evaluations of intelligence: "The ultimate utility and impact of intelligence is generally dependent on the policymakers as consumers."[82]

The Carter Years: An Assessment

The Carter years were a period of increased politicization of intelligence, to some extent as a result of the administration's own views and uses of intelligence, which were characterized by deep internal ideological rifts.[83] Politicization also occurred as a result of the previous investigations and more rigorous oversight. So-called failures received glaring publicity, and even less controversial products and policies became matters of public debate. Such a situation, unique for any intelligence organization, greatly contributed to a certain hesitancy on the part of intelligence producers to express unambiguous views on controversial topics. By and large, the relationship between the intelligence community and the congressional committees often seemed to be better than that between the intelligence community and its primary audience in the executive.[84] It is generally acknowledged, moreover, that far more intelligence leaks occurred among executive branch consumers of intelligence than in Congress.

7

A "Restored" Intelligence Community

During his 1980 election campaign against Jimmy Carter, Ronald Reagan pledged to "restore" the intelligence community, arguing that it had been unduly hampered by restrictions and starved of necessary assets. Political hyperbole aside, it was significant that once again the role of intelligence was seen as a proper election issue, even if only a minor one.[85] That intelligence was once more an issue showed, above all, that intelligence activities could not return to normal after the revelations and investigations. It also showed how the politicizing of intelligence had now become the norm.

DCI Casey

It was not clear what the new administration meant to do to "restore" intelligence beyond increasing its budget. (Actually, the intelligence budget began to increase during the last year of the Carter administration, as did the defense budget. Given his past stance on these issues, however, Carter's action was seen by many as "too little, too late.") It was also not clear whether the incoming Reagan team fully appreciated the changed climate of oversight and what this meant for how they ran the intelligence community.

In December 1980, Reagan named his campaign manager, William Casey, to be DCI.[86] This continued the pattern of replacing the DCI at the beginning of each new administration, which had not been the rule from 1947 to 1977. Casey had hoped to be named secretary of state. Perhaps as compensation, Reagan conferred "cabinet rank" on his new DCI, a move that some questioned. They argued that the president's senior intelligence adviser had no place serving as a member of what was ostensibly a policy-making body.

Casey came to the job with some intelligence experience; he was chief of OSS intelligence operations in Europe during World War II and served on the PFIAB during 1976–1977. His confirmation hearings before the Senate Intelligence Committee – chaired for the first time by a Republican, Senator Barry Goldwater – were not controversial, although two points stood out. First, the senators stressed their oversight role and their expectations of the DCI in that regard. Casey responded with a pledge to "cooperate fully in facilitating the oversight through which Congress can insure that the community operates within the limits of the law." Second, the committee urged Casey to name Admiral Bobby Inman, then director of NSA, to be deputy DCI. Inman had spent most of his naval career in intelligence-related posts and was a great favorite in Congress. The presidential transition team had already made a similar recommendation to Casey, which he had accepted but was now reconsidering. The senators knew this and acted to support Inman, who was, indeed, named deputy DCI, although the unorthodox manner of his nomination did little for his relationship with Casey.[87]

Casey's tenure got off to a rocky start. His choice of Max Hugel, a businessman and campaign contributor, to be DDO, was questioned by many. After a brief and shaky tenure, Hugel resigned. Second, questions arose about Casey's personal finances – specifically, his role in a 1968 stock offering that had been found to be "misleading." After an investigation, the Senate Intelligence Committee voted unanimously in July 1981 that Casey "was not unfit to serve" as DCI.

But the committee also concurred with Casey's statement that the Hugel appointment had been a "mistake."[88]

Among the steps President Reagan took to improve intelligence was restoring the PFIAB to analyze and assess intelligence performance. More controversial were efforts to prepare a new executive order to replace President Carter's. Critics of Carter's E.O. 12036 believed it was too restrictive, framed largely in terms of prohibitions rather than authorizations. On December 4, 1981, President Reagan signed E.O. 12333.[89] Many of Carter's detailed restrictions were rephrased to express permitted activities. The new order also stressed the need to improve intelligence, including several references to competitive analyses among agencies. In several instances the executive order gave permission for covert action in the United States as well as abroad, although not for permission to influence legitimate domestic activities. Furthermore, the right to participate without disclosure in domestic groups was broadened to allow the influencing of the groups' activities under certain circumstances. Limits on the types of information that could be collected were also eased.

By this time, three presidents had issued three different executive orders to govern intelligence in fewer than six years, raising anew the issue of how satisfactory this method was. Reagan's order restored a great deal of flexibility to intelligence, deleting many of the specific organizational and procedural details in the Carter order. Although this method gave each president flexibility, it also ensured impermanence. Nonetheless, the alternative of legislative charters seemed dead. Senate Intelligence Committee chairman Goldwater did not support the concept, nor was there much support elsewhere in the Congress.

Congress focused on other issues. Legislation was reintroduced to enact penalties for the unauthorized disclosure of intelligence agents' identities and to provide some relief for the intelligence community from the Freedom of Information Act (FOIA). Although the act granted an exemption for properly classified national defense and foreign policy information, the CIA and other agencies complained that the requirement to carry out a full search before denying a request had become extremely costly.[90]

During the first session of the 97th Congress, the House Intelligence Committee became involved in a complex investigation into the activities of Edwin Wilson and Frank Terpil. Wilson had worked briefly at CIA and then at a covert branch of the U.S. Navy; Terpil had been at CIA. Their later business activities included selling restricted material and arms to Libya and providing U.S. Army Green Berets to train Libyans with the new equipment. It appeared that Wilson and Terpil had made use of their former intelligence roles in their activities and that some former colleagues had given them assistance as well. Wilson was arrested in 1982, was convicted on several counts, and sentenced to 32 years in connection with his Libyan activities. (He was subsequently sentenced to an additional 25 years for conspiracy to murder those responsible for his prosecution and conviction.) Terpil, who was last seen in Beirut, was widely presumed to be dead, although subsequent reports have mentioned him as still being active in Cuba, Libya, Southeast Asia, and former Warsaw Pact nations.[91] The Wilson-Terpil case raised a number of serious issues, including the degree to which the activities of former intelligence employees could be limited or controlled, the relationship between former and current employees, and the inadequacies in the laws governing technology transfer.

The Reagan Doctrine

One aspect of foreign relations that probably contributed to Reagan's election was the growing sense of embattlement that many Americans felt as they surveyed the world. It was not only the humiliation inflicted in Iran, but the various Soviet successes in such Third World countries as Cambodia (through Vietnamese surrogates), Ethiopia (which was more of a trade with the United States for Somalia), Angola (through its Cuban expeditionary force), Afghanistan, and Nicaragua.

The new administration wished to combat this trend and hoped to reverse it,[92] initially by continuing aid to the Afghan mujahidin and supporting the contras in Nicaragua. Yet the two largely overt programs – at least in terms of their existence if not in actual levels of support – were treated very differently by both the administration and Congress. Afghanistan represented a clear case of Soviet aggression from the outside and involved clearly defined aims – that is, denying the Soviets control of the country and eventually forcing their withdrawal. The Afghan program did not face substantial opposition in Congress.

The internal situation in Nicaragua, however, was not as clear, given that the contras were fighting fellow Nicaraguans, who had Soviet and Cuban support. Nor were the administration's goals clear. When the contra project began in 1981, the stated goal was to stem Sandinista arms to leftist insurgents in neighboring El Salvador. By 1983–1984, the goal had expanded to the creating of sufficient pressure on the Sandinista regime to force it to democratize internally and negotiate a regional settlement with its neighbors.

Although Congress voted funds for the contras in 1981 and 1982, some qualms were already there, most evident in the 1982 amendment offered by House Intelligence Committee Chairman Edward Boland. This first Boland amendment stipulated that the covert military aid being voted for the next fiscal year could not be used to overthrow the Sandinista government. By late 1983 there was strong opposition in the Democratic-controlled House.

A key event for Congress was the mining of the harbor in Corinto, Nicaragua by the CIA in early 1984, which Casey initially tried to pass off as an independent contra operation. When he admitted the CIA role, the effect in the Senate Intelligence Committee was devastating. Senator Goldwater fired off a blistering letter to the DCI.[93] Casey argued that the operation had been briefed to the committee, but the reference was so minor and oblique that the committee's vice chairman, Senator Daniel Moynihan, resigned in protest over what he viewed as a contravention of the new oversight provisions.[94]

The immediate result of this episode was the negotiation of the "Casey accords." Formally signed by Casey, with the president's approval, and the Senate Intelligence Committee on June 6, 1984, the DCI agreed to provide the committee with all Presidential Findings for all covert actions (including changes to ongoing ones) and prior notice before they were implemented, as well as regular progress and status reviews.[95]

The more long-lasting result was the squandering of whatever trust Congress had in Casey. In a compromise with the Senate, contra funding for 1984 was capped at a level below the contras' expected needs and recourse to the DCI's contingency reserve fund was precluded.[96] Given the amount already spent that year, the contras were now out of funds. Later in 1984 the Senate joined the House in opposing further funding for the contras unless certain conditions were met.[97] These were embodied in the second Boland amendment, which denied any Defense Department, CIA, or other U.S. intelligence agency funds to the contras without a prior vote of Congress.

In his second inaugural address, in January 1985, President Reagan gave greater definition to this overall policy, stating his commitment to the "freedom fighters" in Afghanistan, Angola, Cambodia, and Nicaragua. Again, in terms of public support, Afghanistan was not controversial. Indeed, the decision in 1986–1987 to provide the mujahidin with Stinger antiaircraft missiles had a telling effect on the conduct of the war, causing the Soviets to abandon hitherto successful tactics.

In Angola, Congress reversed itself, voting in 1985 to repeal the Clark amendment that had prohibited aid to the UNITA guerrillas without Congress's approval. In Cambodia, with its tangle of factions – the Hanoi-backed regime, the brutal Khmer Rouge (which reverted to the jungle after its ouster), and the Non-Communist Resistance or NCR—Congress led the way with aid for the NCR.

Once again, Nicaragua was the sticking point. Although Congress had approved nonlethal or humanitarian aid to the contras, with a prohibition on CIA or Defense Department disbursement, much of 1985 was taken up with continuing debates and maneuvering over whether actually to release the funds. This was not accomplished until mid-summer. In 1986, President Reagan campaigned forcefully for $100 million in aid to the contras, $70 million of which was military. In a stunning reversal, Congress voted the aid that summer. These various funds were subject to the third Boland amendment, which specified the types of assistance the covered agencies could provide. By the fall, however, this was all overtaken by the revelation of the Iran-contra operation.

By the end of the Reagan administration, at least two of these anti-Soviet ventures had been successful. The mujahidin fought the Soviets to a standstill, and they withdrew their combat forces from Afghanistan. In Angola, the United States negotiated the withdrawal of South Africans and Cubans. But the reasons for these successes likely lie beyond covert aid and are difficult to untangle. Providing Stingers in Afghanistan certainly represented a military turning point. It is also important to distinguish between the actual military aid provided in these largely overt "covert" actions and their broader political significance. These operations came after a period of U.S. withdrawal and pronounced self-doubt. The very fact that the United States was willing to reengage Soviet expansion and Soviet surrogates in this way may have been just as important to the ultimately successful outcome as was the amount or type of assistance provided to the mujahidin, UNITA, or the contras. Yet, it cannot be discerned whether these U.S.-backed operations increased Soviet costs so much that reversal was necessary, or whether reversal resulted from largely independent calculations made by Mikhail Gorbachev about the

Soviet Union's own domestic and international needs. Finally, such policies, even when successful, entail a political cost, given that many Americans and many U.S. allies have always been uncomfortable with this aspect of U.S. intelligence policy.

The Year of the Spy

Nineteen eighty-five brought a series of revelations about serious, hostile espionage activities carried out by U.S. citizens, leading many to dub it "the year of the spy." The revelations actually began in October 1984, with the arrest of Samuel Loring Morison, a Navy intelligence analyst, who passed classified reconnaissance satellite photographs of a Soviet naval shipyard to the British publication *Jane's Defence Weekly*, for which he occasionally wrote. The successful prosecution under the espionage statute raised some controversy, with some arguing that a leak to the press was not espionage.[98] Morison was sentenced to two years.

The day after Morison's arrest, Richard Miller, an FBI agent, was arrested and charged with espionage, the first FBI agent so charged. Miller, a lackluster agent, admitted having an affair with Soviet emigré Svetlana Ogorodonikov, who was arrested along with her husband. After an initial mistrial, Miller was sentenced to life.

More sensational was the arrest of the so-called Walker spy ring in May 1985. John Walker, a retired navy chief warrant officer, his son Michael, then a navy seaman, and John's, brother Arthur, also a navy retiree, were all arrested and charged with espionage. Two weeks later, Jerry Whitworth, a former shipmate of John's, was also arrested. It turned out that John Walker had been passing crucial cryptographic information to the Soviet Union for over 17 years, raising troubling questions about U.S. counterintelligence capabilities. Indeed, the tipoff to the Walker ring came from John's former wife, without whom it might have remained unnoticed even longer.[99] John Walker was sentenced to two concurrent life sentences, Michael to 25 years, Arthur to life, and Whitworth to 365 years.

In July 1985, Sharon Scranage, a CIA clerk once posted to Ghana, was arrested along with her Ghanaian lover, Michael Soussoudis, to whom she had revealed CIA methods and informants, some of whom were apparently killed. She was sentenced to five years, later reduced to two; he was sentenced to 20 years, but was immediately exchanged for some Ghanaians who had allegedly worked for the United States.

In September 1985, former CIA employee Edward Lee Howard eluded FBI surveillance in New Mexico and disappeared. Howard had reportedly been trained by the DDO for posting to Moscow (as had his wife) to deal with Soviet citizens who were U.S. agents. Howard's initial CIA polygraph had indicated drug use, but this was not seen as an ongoing problem. A later exam revealed drug and alcohol abuse, marital problems, and petty theft. Faced with the dilemma of shifting Howard to a less sensitive post where he would still be a security risk or letting him go altogether and risking the effects of his disgruntlement, the CIA chose the latter. Howard was later charged with passing information to the Soviets that allowed them to arrest U.S. sources and to expel U.S. intelligence personnel from the embassy in Moscow, effectively hobbling U.S. activities there.[100] In the late summer of 1986, Howard resurfaced in Moscow, where he had reportedly been given political asylum.

In November 1985, Jonathan Jay Pollard, a navy intelligence analyst, and his wife Anne were arrested outside the Israeli embassy in Washington, D.C., apparently seeking asylum. Pollard was convicted of passing documents to Israel and sentenced to life; his wife was sentenced to five years.[101] Four Israelis were unindicted co-conspirators. Although the Israeli government claimed this was a rogue operation, many found this difficult to believe given the scope of the material and the amount Pollard was paid.

Larry Wu-Tai Chin, a former CIA cmployee, was arrested the day after the Pollards. He was convicted of having passed documents to China for more than 30 years, but committed suicide before sentencing. Chin's case raised questions about CIA counterintelligence practices and the reliability of the periodic security reviews of employees.

Finally, Ronald Pelton, a former NSA employee, was also arrested in November 1985. Pelton confessed to having passed to the Soviets extremely sensitive information regarding U.S. interceptions of their communications over the past five years. He was sentenced to life imprisonment.

This seeming barrage of cases raised serious questions about U.S. counterintelligence capabilities. In the cases of the Walker ring and Pelton, the motives were money, and there had been indications of financial problems that could have aroused suspicion. Pollard was motivated by a desire to help Israel, and by money, but had done little to conceal his activities. Howard's unreliability should have been flagged earlier. But given the large number of people in the United States holding sensitive clearances (over 5 million in 1985, according to the House Intelligence Committee), it is difficult, if not impossible, to keep track of all of them and to spot these indications of potential problems. Moreover, the Chin case showed that even periodic rechecks of personnel were imperfect. The overall impression was that counterintelligence efforts were either too small or too weak or both.

Interestingly, in 1985 there was also a U.S. counterintelligence coup that turned into a disaster and was closely related to two of these cases, Pelton and Howard. In July 1985, Vitaly Yurchenko, security officer for all Soviet operations in North America, defected. He not only named Soviet agents, identifying Pelton and referring to another agent less directly (an agent eventually identified as Howard), but also disclosed much about Soviet methodology and techniques – the "tradecraft" of spies.

Yurchenko could not have come at a better time, seemingly offsetting all of these intelligence losses. Casey used Yurchenko's defection avidly with Congress. But in November 1985, Yurchenko walked away from his CIA companion in a Washington restaurant and redefected, an event the Soviet Union understandably publicized. As is often the case with defectors, Yurchenko felt alienated from his new home and missed the high-level attention he had received when he had first come over. His return to the Soviet Union was a tremendous embarrassment, causing some to question Yurchenko's authenticity – in which most experts and observers continued to believe – and leading to new questions about CIA counterintelligence and its ability to deal with defectors.[102]

These various cases led to a series of executive branch reviews (the Stilwell Commission in Defense and the Inman Panel in State, as well as a CIA reexamination of its procedures for handling defectors). The Senate and House Intelligence committees both held hearings on counterintelligence problems and issued reports.[103] Both committees found flaws in screening and hiring practices and excessive reliance on polygraphs; insufficient reinvestigation of previously cleared employees; cynicism about an overly large, complex, and unwieldy classification system; and disorganization in the counterintelligence community.

The Iran-Contra Affair

The so-called Iran-contra affair was really the merging of three policy threads.[104] The first arose directly from the Reagan Doctrine – that is, support for the contras in the face of Congress's express opposition. The other two threads were an interest in improving relations with Iran, with an eye toward the post-Khomeini period, and concern over U.S. citizens (including CIA Beirut station chief William Buckley) being held hostage in Lebanon.

In brief, during the period in which funds for the contras were cut, President Reagan urged the NSC staff to help the contras "keep body and soul together." To a large extent, this was done through private fund raising and contributions by foreign governments, as well as the use of privately owned logistics assets – the so-called off-the-shelf covert action capability that NSC staffer Lt. Col. Oliver North said Casey had approved. Those involved would later argue that this did not violate the Boland amendment's prohibition on any Defense, CIA, or intelligence agency funds going to the contras without prior congressional approval, because neither the NSC nor its staff were part of Defense, CIA, or an intelligence agency.

At roughly the same time, there was also concern within the NSC staff about post-Khomeini Iran and any potential Soviet advantage. This led to a June–July 1985 proposal to improve relations immediately, beginning with an end to the military embargo against Iran. This staff concept was killed by the strong objections of Secretary of State George Shultz and Secretary of Defense Caspar Weinberger.

Israel's interest in its own relations with Iran, a former major arms customer, allowed the concept to be revived and expanded, although now it was largely, but not entirely, self-contained within the NSC staff, under the successive National Security Advisers Robert McFarlane and Vice Admiral John Poindexter. Manucher Ghorbanifar, an Iranian who claimed to have ties to "moderates" in Tehran, suggested swapping arms for hostages. Two shipments of TOW antitank missiles from Israel to Iran, to be replenished by the United States, were made that summer; one hostage was released.[105] A Presidential Finding authorizing such activity was written retroactively and not reported to Congress.

Another delivery was made in February 1986. In April, North, who had been working the contra problem initially but was now involved in Iranian issues as well, suggested diverting profits from the sales to Iran into the contra project. In May, a U.S. delegation, headed by McFarlane – who was no longer on the NSC staff – undertook an abortive trip to Tehran to meet the "moderates." There were several more arms shipments to Iran; one more hostage was released.

In November 1986, *Al-Shira'*, a Lebanese publication, first revealed the McFarlane trip, which Iran confirmed, creating a political crisis in the United States. President Reagan sought unsuccessfully to explain that he had not traded arms for hostages, something he had vowed never to do, but was simply seeking political openings in Tehran. Finally, Reagan asked Attorney General Edwin Meese to find out exactly what had been going on. Meese's investigation discovered the diversion of funds to the contras.

On December 1, 1986, Reagan appointed a Special Review Board, chaired by former Senator John Tower, along with former Senator and Secretary of State Edmund Muskie and former National Security Adviser Scowcroft, "to review activities of the National Security Council." Working quickly through case studies of every administration since Truman's and through interviews—except for Poindexter and North, who both declined—the board reported on February 26, 1987.[106]

The Special Review Board believed the major problem was that these initiatives were not conducted within regular channels; their covert nature allowed policies to be conducted that were contradictory to administration goals or congressional mandates. It also found that the executive branch ignored intelligence oversight requirements in its internal operations and in failing to keep Congress informed and faulted President Reagan's personal management style. The board, however, saw no need for major changes in the role or function of the national security adviser or the NSC staff. It laid out a model for the NSC staff that it believed would improve supervision and the monitoring of activities, but recognized the unique nature of the NSC staff as an extremely malleable organization that should be able to respond to the differing needs and working methods of each president.

As the effects of the revelations were building, DCI Casey suffered a cerebral seizure and was diagnosed with a brain tumor. (He had earlier been treated secretly for prostate cancer.) Casey resigned as DCI on January 29, 1987, and his deputy, Robert Gates, was nominated to replace him. Casey died in May 1987.[107]

Gates was the first career CIA officer from the "analytical side of the house" to be nominated as DCI. Inevitably, his nomination was caught up in the Iran-contra affair. Gates maintained that as deputy DCI he had not been involved in the affair, but admitted that he could have been more aggressive in pursuing the first indications when they were made known to him. He denied that he slanted intelligence analysis to support policy or helped Casey prepare misleading testimony on Iran-contra. In the face of growing opposition in the Senate, however, Gates withdrew his nomination in March 1987, becoming the second DCI nominee in 10 years to suffer that fate. In May 1987, Judge William Webster, director of the FBI, was nominated to be DCI and was quickly confirmed.

Iran-contra dominated the news during the summer of 1987 as select House and Senate committees held unprecedented joint public hearings. It is difficult to summarize the findings of the committees, given the numerous minority and individual views that were taken in the final report.[108] The majority found a "seriously" flawed policy process, inappropriate activities by the NSC staff, lack of accountability, failure to comply with executive or congressional oversight provisions for covert actions, and evasion of the Boland amendments. They called for much stricter legislative requirements for covert actions, creation of a statutory CIA inspector general, and strengthening of Congress's oversight capabilities. The minority strongly disagreed with these findings and recommendations, concentrating instead on steps to improve security and to restore the president's power in foreign policy against such legislative vehicles as the Boland amendments.

Several different intelligence-related issues came to the fore in Iran-contra. First was the struggle between the president and Congress over covert aid to the contras. Congressional support waxed and waned between 1981 and 1986; this internal struggle left alive the administration's hope that if the contras could be sustained long enough – even if the means were dubious – Congress might reverse itself. At the same time, the mining of the Nicaraguan harbor of Corinto planted in the minds of many in Congress the impression that Casey might not respect oversight rules or even limited legislative restrictions. Those who opposed the contra project outright were joined by those left uneasy by Casey, thus the Boland amendments. The argument that the NSC staff was not covered by these restrictions was, at best, disingenuous. The operational role played by the NSC staff was a serious departure from what most people understood to be the NSC's policy coordination function. It also gravely short-circuited both that proper role and executive branch oversight.

Second, the prolonged contra debate renewed the issue of the inflexibility of paramilitary operations. Once an armed group has been organized and put in the field, policy choices begin to narrow significantly. In the end there are usually two options: continue the struggle indefinitely, regardless of the chances for success, or abandon the surrogate force, regardless of the promises that have been made. Pursuing middle ground, as in the case of the contras – that is, providing sufficient nonlethal aid to keep the contras alive but not fighting – ultimately is not viable. Inevitably, the decision comes back to the starker alternatives.

Finally, Iran-contra renewed the issue as to how the components of the executive branch assess such operations once they are under way, reflecting the old bifurcation between intelligence operations and analysis. It is doubtful that many senior officials in the Reagan administration wanted to see the Sandinistas stay in power. But this desire was not necessarily consonant with supporting the contras. Indeed, some intelligence analysts questioned, on the basis of available intelligence, whether the contras could win. For policymakers who supported the contras wholeheartedly – and perhaps more emotionally than analytically – this was seen as disloyalty, leading them to question the motives of the intelligence analysts.[109]

Congressional Oversight, 1986–1989

The counterintelligence setbacks and the wearying debate over the contras, even in advance of Iran-contra, led to an especially difficult period in the intelligence community's relations with Congress. In 1985, Senator Dave Durenberger succeeded Barry Goldwater as chairman of the Senate Intelligence Committee. By the end of the year Durenberger and Casey had engaged in an exchange of corrosive public letters via the press, in which the DCI accused Congress of leaks that had hurt operations, sources, and methods, and the chairman charged that Casey and the entire community lacked direction, an overall strategy, and an understanding of the Soviet Union. Senators Patrick Leahy and Jesse Helms, on opposite sides of the political spectrum, raised criticisms of their own.[110] The various revelations of Iran-contra fueled an already hostile atmosphere.

A key concern for Congress was enacting legislation to prevent a repeat of Iran-contra, heightened by executive branch assertions that current law gave the president wide latitude in covert action.[111] Several bills were introduced in the 100th Congress (1987–1988), including among their proposals a fixed term for the DCI; bans on operational intelligence activity by the NSC; creation of the permanent, statutory position of CIA inspector general; and audits of CIA financial transactions, programs, and activities by the comptroller general (that is, the General Accounting Office). Although none of these proposals was enacted by the end of the Reagan administration, the details of one—the Senate Intelligence Committee's oversight bill (S. 1721, 100th Congress)—became significant. This bill was introduced after prolonged negotiations between the committee and the executive over new procedures for oversight in light of abuses found in Iran-contra.[112] It clearly placed responsibility for keeping the Senate and House Intelligence committees "fully and currently informed" on the president, not on the DCI and other agency heads. The president would also be responsible for reporting illegal activities or significant failures, again transferring this from the DCI. S. 1721 gave the first explicit statutory authority for "special activities." It required that all Presidential Findings be submitted in writing (with certain limited exceptions) and prohibited their being issued retroactively; it also required them to be reported to Congress within 48 hours and to specify all U.S. agencies authorized to participate, as well as any third party or third country participants. S. 1721 passed the Senate but was not reported to the House floor.

Counterintelligence concerns continued to be an issue, focusing now on the U.S. embassy in Moscow. In January 1987, the Marine Corps revealed that a Marine guard who had served at the embassy, Clayton Lonetree, had been confined on suspicion of espionage. Lonetree confessed to having an affair with a Soviet woman and to providing classified documents to the Soviets. Another Marine guard, Arnold Bracy, was also found to have had an affair with a Soviet woman ("swallows" in intelligence parlance); he confessed to espionage with Lonetree but later recanted. The main fear was that the marines had allowed Soviets unimpeded access to secure areas in the embassy, which a CIA-NSA study reportedly confirmed.[113]

Early in 1987, it was also discovered that the new U.S. chancery building under construction in Moscow was honeycombed with various eavesdropping devices. This added to an older controversy concerning the various agreements of the late 1960s and early 1970s concerning new U.S. and Soviet embassies. Critics in the United States were already concerned about the fact that the Soviet site in Washington was on a high piece of ground (Mount Alto), enhancing any eavesdropping capabilities, and that Soviet workers were used to build the U.S. site in Moscow.

At the request of Secretary Shultz, former DCI and Secretary of defense James Schlesinger surveyed the Moscow site, concluding that it was filled with listening devices and that the top three floors should be dismantled and rebuilt by the United States along with the construction of a new annex to house sensitive facilities.[114] By 1991 the issue of the embassy was still unresolved, with the executive and Congress both wavering between "Tear Down" (razing the old building and replacing it entirely) and "Top Hat" (demolishing the upper floor and adding three new secure floors). In October 1991, Congress authorized funds for a new U.S. embassy in Moscow, but did not choose among "Tear Down," "Top Hat," or building an adjacent structure, leaving that to the executive. A dramatic footnote to the Moscow embassy issue came in December 1991, when then-head of the KGB Vadim Bakatin admitted to U.S. Ambassador Robert Strauss that the new building had been bugged and also provided what he said were detailed plans of the bugging.[115]

Gorbachev and the New Demands of Arms Control

Mikhail Gorbachev's ascension to power in 1985 led to a series of political changes that created wholly new intelligence challenges. Despite 40 years of practice, the intelligence community's art of Kremlinology had not advanced very far. Initially, most U.S. analysts were as skeptical of the changes that Gorbachev promised as was the average Soviet citizen, who had heard much the same theme at the outset of each new regime. But when Gorbachev decided, for both internal and external reasons, to emphasize the reaching of arms control agreements with the United States, the results for U.S. intelligence were significant.

The Reagan administration, skeptical of Soviet intentions and their past arms control compliance practices, sought to raise the standards for acceptable verification in new agreements, stressing a new standard of "effective" rather than the previous "adequate." It emphasized the role of on-site inspection, raised by some as a sine qua non despite its limited role in improving verification and advocated by other policy officials largely as a means of precluding agreements, assuming the Soviets would balk.

Even as negotiations over intermediate and strategic nuclear forces (the Intermediate-Range Nuclear Force or

INF talks and the Strategic Arms Reduction Talks or START) progressed, the Reagan administration begin issuing annual reports on Soviet noncompliance in 1984. Each report raised significant questions about Soviet reliability, thus also raising the issue of how the United States could be negotiating with them at the same time. In February 1985, the United States formally charged the Soviets with violating the Antiballistic Missile (ABM) treaty by constructing a radar at Krasnoyarsk.[116] Moreover, the compliance report process proved stressful for intelligence-policy relations, pitting intelligence officials, who were hesitant to make judgments beyond available evidence, against policy officials, who needed no convincing that the Soviets were systematically cheating.

In 1987, the United States and USSR agreed on the INF treaty, eliminating this entire class of weapons. The completion of START did not seem, at the time, very far off. INF included a number of on-site inspection requirements, including the posting of inspectors in each other's countries permanently at one missile production site. This immediately raised new counterintelligence concerns, and for the first time, the FBI became an active participant in U.S. arms control deliberations.

At the same, these new treaties would place additional burdens on always scarce National Technical Means, an area of concern for Congress. The House Intelligence Committee found NTM research and development to be fragmented and unfocused.[117] The Senate Intelligence Committee, in its consideration of the INF treaty, questioned how INF and START would affect NTM capabilities and called for funds "to initiate a long-term program to modernize and improve upon current plans for intelligence collection."[118] The committee reportedly attached an informal understanding to the INF treaty (known as the Boren-Cohen Initiative after the chairman and vice chairman), requiring the annual launching of additional imagery satellites. The administration resisted, concerned that this would strain the intelligence budget if the funds had to be found within current resources. The Senate Intelligence Committee in effect held consideration of the INF treaty hostage until the Reagan administration compromised, agreeing to increased NTM funding, albeit below the Senate's original level.

Assessment

True to his campaign pledge, Ronald Reagan had given greater prominence and freedom to the intelligence community. Because of Casey's access to the president and his questionable role as a policy advocate, the intelligence community – or at least the CIA – rose in significance to a level perhaps unequalled since the days of Allen Dulles. Morale in the community improved, not only in operations but in analysis, where Casey made some positive moves, giving stronger emphasis, for example, to agencies' disagreements over analytical issues rather than seeking blandly worded compromises.

As in other areas, however, Reagan's remote management style – the setting of broad goals with little interest in how they were achieved – depended heavily on the skill and judgment of subordinates at various levels. As Iran-contra showed, this approach could be especially dangerous in covert actions, whose very nature and the highly compartmentalized manner in which they were customarily handled could permit potentially grave abuses of authority and law.

One must also view the Reagan years in the context of the years immediately preceding them – a period of humiliation and near-siege mentality for the United States abroad. The Reagan Doctrine, despite its vagueness, seemingly offered an end to this period in terms not heard since the Eisenhower and Kennedy administrations. But in assessing the actual efficacy of U.S. covert programs, it becomes difficult, if not impossible, to discern to what degree they were successful in and of themselves and to what degree successful because they came at a time when the Soviet leadership wanted or had to curtail its overseas ventures. As some have argued, U.S. efforts may have contributed to this Soviet necessity, but we cannot yet be sure.

Even if these programs were successful, they continued to exact a domestic price for the United States. Little about these programs was truly covert, either in terms of their actual existence or the approximate levels of funding. But as the long debate over the contras showed, a significant segment of the political leadership had problems with at least certain covert actions, although it was sometimes difficult to fathom why supporting the mujahidin was acceptable and supporting the contras was not. Aside from the merits of the debate on either side, the Reagan administration (especially DCI Casey) failed, much to its own peril, to be attentive to Congress's intelligence oversight requirements. Even before Iran-contra broke in late 1986, relations were strained, especially with the Senate committee. Casey may have been able to turn back the clock to a freer time for intelligence, but he could not do this with Congress, a fact that he never seemed to grasp.

8

Intelligence in the Post–Cold War World

In January 1989, George Bush was inaugurated as president, the first former DCI to accede to that position. Within 10 months of his inaugural, the entire post–World War II order in Europe collapsed, with the Soviet Union acquiescing to the peaceful dismantlement of its satellite empire and to the reunification of Germany. At the same time, the power of the Soviet Union itself diminished daily as its economic system neared collapse and its political system struggled between those favoring ever more rapid steps toward more responsive and more democratic government and those clinging to the older levers of control. Nine months after the collapse of the old order in Europe, Saddam Hussein invaded Kuwait; five months later Iraq was forcibly ejected by a broad United Nations (UN) coalition largely formed and led by the United States. In August 1991, Soviet hardliners staged an abortive coup against Gorbachev, which in turn led to the rapid demise of Communist control and the eventual dissolution of the USSR into its component and now separate republics. In this rush of dramatic events the role played by the intelligence community and its future were both questioned, even as Congress and the president continued to cope with oversight issues stemming from Iran-contra.

The Oversight Struggle, 1989–1991

There was some irony in the fact that it fell to former DCI George Bush to come to terms with the oversight issues left unresolved after Iran-contra. The first reform issue to reach fruition was the creation of the position of CIA inspector general. Despite vigorous opposition from the Bush administration (supported publicly by former DCIs Helms and Schlesinger), Congress created the position in 1989, making it subject to Senate confirmation and having the inspector general report directly to the DCI. The House Intelligence Committee had also wanted Congress to have access to all of the inspector general's reports, which the administration and Republican members of the committee opposed. A compromise procedure was created: requests for reports would have to come from the leadership of the Senate and House Intelligence committees, not from individual members; under some circumstances, the CIA could provide a summary, rather than the entire report, although each committee could demand the full report if it found the summary inadequate.

Instead of reintroducing a bill with the provisions of S. 1721, the Senate Intelligence Committee opened negotiations with the Bush administration on the 48-hour reporting provision. After some nine months of unresolved discussions, the committee attached the 48-hour requirement to the annual intelligence authorization bill. As hoped, this elicited a response from President Bush, who sent letters to both committees recognizing their disagreement with the Justice Department's open-ended formulation in 1986 about "timely fashion" and pledging to give prior notice whenever possible or to delay it by no more than "a few days." But Bush also cited a constitutional prerogative to withhold notice even longer.[119]

Much of the 1990 congressional debate over intelligence centered on the continued funding of UNITA in Angola, to which many in the House objected. The Senate Intelligence Committee again inserted its oversight concepts into the authorization bill, although without the 48-hour rule, expecting that this would bring a presidential veto. Some in the House felt that the Senate's draft left the president with too much discretion in allowing Findings to be reported in a "timely fashion." Much to Congress's surprise, President Bush used a pocket veto on the bill (he refused to sign it after Congress had adjourned) – the first time this had ever happened to an intelligence authorization. In his veto message, Bush cited two main objections: first, the definition of covert action included U.S. requests to foreign governments or private citizens, a category that the president believed was ill-defined, would constrain sensitive discussions between U.S. diplomats and foreigners, and would deter foreign governments from holding certain discussions; second, the "Joint Explanatory Statement" accompanying the legislation apparently interpreted "timely fashion" to mean "in a few days," which Bush considered an infringement on his authority.[120]

Beyond signaling continued disagreement on oversight, Bush's veto raised a new issue, as reported by the two Intelligence committees to the president – the requirement of the National Security Act that there be a specific authorization for funding intelligence activities. The Bush administration argued that the defense authorization bill was sufficient because intelligence funds ultimately were part of the defense bill. The committees vowed to reopen the entire issue in 1991, which they did. They now made some changes to the bill, however, to meet the president's objections: discussions with foreign countries still had to be reported, but the country in question did not have to be named; the legislative report accompanying the bill also noted that a majority of members believed "in a timely fashion" meant "in a few days," but recognized the president's right to assert he could delay longer.

Thus, over four years after the first revelation of Iran-contra, its major identified abuses (oral Findings, ex post facto Findings, delayed notification to Congress, loopholes concerning U.S. government agencies not clearly part of the intelligence community) were addressed, and covert action was finally given a definition in law.[121]

In July 1991, President Bush and Congress agreed on the new bill, which became law on August 15, 1991. In a written statement accompanying the law, however, Bush took exception to the definition of covert action, saying that it was unnecessary and infringed on his powers, particularly with regard to military activities.

The Debate over Post–Cold War Intelligence

Few could argue with the contention that the intelligence community owed much of its creation to the cold war or that its primary preoccupation for those 40-plus years had been the Soviet Union. With the Soviet threat substantially dissipated, many asked if this were not the time to rethink the community's focus and organization. Among the issues cited as needing more attention were narcotics, weapons proliferation, and economic intelligence.

The problems raised by narcotics and weapons proliferation and the intelligence support required to counter them were fairly well defined, although somewhat frustrating for policymakers because they are not easily susceptible to U.S. power or influence. In economics, the intelligence issues were very different. First, the desire to emphasize economics seemed to ignore the fact that for years the various components had collected and produced a great deal of economic intelligence. Second, it was also unclear as to what was missing or how it would be used. The major area of concern was what was seen as declining U.S. ability to compete with Japan, Germany, and other countries. But few seemed able to define how improved collection or analysis would address this problem, given the absence of close industry-government ties in the United States comparable to those of its economic rivals, the risks inherent in revealing highly classified information to private industry, or how and to which industries such information might be disseminated. Some critics of this entire approach believed it represented a desire for some "magic bullet" cure for economic problems rather than a willingness to make the hard choices that might be necessary on such issues as spending, taxes, deficits, education, and industrial policy.

Even before the collapse of the Warsaw Pact and the Soviet Union, it was clear that the intelligence community would not continue to have available to it the large funding increases it had received since 1980. The diminished Soviet threat added impetus to this trend as well as to efforts to scale down the overall size of intelligence agencies. A major target for such efforts were the various Defense intelligence entities – not only the DIA, but the individual service and command intelligence units. Congress put the Defense Department on notice that redundancies had to be consolidated or eliminated. The House and Senate Armed Services committees mandated annual 5 percent reductions in DIA for the fiscal years 1992–1996, to which the House Intelligence Committee objected. In 1991, as part of its budget authorization process, the Senate Armed Services Committee drafted statutory legislation for the DIA, largely to protect the agency from what it saw as policy encroachment by the responsible assistant secretary of defense, who had implemented a defense intelligence restructuring earlier that year.

In 1991 the Senate Intelligence Committee also proposed making public the aggregate intelligence budget (the National Foreign Intelligence Program or NFIP, and Defense's Tactical Intelligence and Related Activities or TIARA), arguing that release of the figures would give the public a better understanding of the costs of foreign intelligence and would increase public involvement in the national debate over resource allocation without harming national security.[122] The basic issues were the same as they had been in 1977, pitting concerns about the public's right to know how public funds were being spent against security concerns and questions about whether releasing these large aggregate figures would actually give the public any real basis for judging how well or poorly their tax dollars were being spent.

The Gulf War

Saddam Hussein's invasion of Kuwait in August 1990 and the subsequent war raised new questions about U.S. intelligence capabilities. To what degree did the intelligence community foresee the Iraqi invasion and warn policymakers? This question raised a second, perhaps more significant, question: Would better intelligence have made a difference? Critics of the intelligence community's performance argued that warnings of an Iraqi invasion came too late. DCI Webster admitted that the community had recognized Saddam's aggressive tendencies, but believed the war with Iran had left Iraq too tired and weak to try a new venture. Webster also noted now difficult it was to know what Saddam—or anyone else—was thinking.[123] But this statement served to support those critics who continued to believe that U.S. intelligence concentrated too much on technical collection and not enough on human intelligence.[124]

The question as to whether better intelligence on Iraqi intentions would have changed the situation suggested a slightly different picture. First, U.S policymakers would have had to accept the reversal of a policy that was either positive toward Iraq or ignored certain provocations. Second, the United States would have had to find a means of deterring Iraq, most likely through some level of threat. But little that subsequently happened to Iraq—the sanctions and effective embargo, the 30-nation alliance, and Saudi acceptance of a massive foreign military presence—was thinkable, credible, or even possible without the Iraqi invasion. Nor was there any likelihood that Saddam Hussein, surrounded by sycophants and not seriously thwarted in the past, would believe these threats. Whatever the shortcomings of U.S. intelligence in the period before the invasion of Kuwait, it remains uncertain that it necessarily would have led to a policy that would have deterred Saddam Hussein.

Intelligence performance during the war raised different issues, voiced primarily by Desert Storm commander General Norman Schwarzkopf. He was mainly concerned about the analyses and estimates being produced in Washington that were heavily hedged, filled with disclaimers, and of particularly little use to him; the differences in battlefield assessments in Washington and in the theater and an overall collection system more attuned to "national" tasks than to theater requirements; and the difficulties that service intelligence units had in sharing intelligence because of incompatible technical systems. An interim report prepared by the Defense Department supported many of these concerns, particularly the organization of joint intelligence support for field commands, better theater access to information from national intelligence technical collection systems, and the issue of bomb damage assessment.[125]

In late 1991, the Intelligence committees continued to study the issues raised by the Gulf War. The Senate Armed Service Committee, as part of its draft charter for the DIA, proposed centralizing management of satellite imagery in that agency in response to concerns over intelligence support to combat, an organizational concept also supported by the Senate Intelligence Committee, which further proposed that the deputy director of the National Photographic Interpretation Center (NPIC) alternate every three years between the CIA and the Defense Department. This committee also wanted to put greater emphasis on human intelligence resources and broader access to that class of information. The committee proposed that the CIA create an assistant DDO (ADDO) who would be selected by the secretary of defense from among flag-rank officers; this ADDO would improve Defense Department liaison with the DDO and ensure that military requirements for human intelligence were represented earlier and more forcefully.[126] By early 1992, such an ADDO position had been created by the DCI.

The rapid drumbeat of events in Eastern Europe and the Gulf left many wondering about overall U.S. intelligence capabilities. Some of the debate surfaced in the hearings over Robert Gates's second nomination to be DCI. The public criticism moved Richard J. Kerr, acting DCI, to write a rare letter to the *New York Times* publicly defending CIA analysis on the fall of the Berlin Wall, the intentions of Saddam Hussein, and the collapse of the Soviet Union. Kerr went so far as to quote from recent analyses and argued against the "simplistic criteria of 'success or failure'" as it "trivialized" the role of intelligence.[127]

Reprise: Robert Gates and Iran-Contra

DCI Webster's future became a subject of speculation as soon as Bush took office. Unlike his two predecessors, however, Bush did not replace the DCI as part of his new team.[128] Nonetheless, rumors continued to surface about Webster's imminent departure. Whatever Bush's intentions, Webster's position improved after the collapse of the Soviet satellites at the end of 1989. The DCI appeared to be much more eager to accept the likely positive implications of this change than was Secretary of Defense Dick Cheney, a difference that gained Webster supporters in Congress.

Critics believed Webster's grasp of the substance of the issues to be less than his predecessor's. Yet Webster brought to his job a clear sense of things that needed to be done to regain ground lost because of Casey's relations with Congress and the effects of Iran-contra. Few also appreciated how difficult it must have been to be a DCI serving a president not only extremely knowledgeable about foreign affairs but also a former DCI himself. Indeed, Bush continued to take an active interest in intelligence, including having access to "raw" products during moments of crisis.[129]

In May 1991, Webster announced his retirement. President Bush nominated Robert Gates, now serving as deputy national security adviser, to be DCI. The initial signs in the

Senate for Gates's second nomination appeared favorable. Whatever doubts about his knowledge of or involvement in Iran-contra that had proved fatal in 1987 had apparently been resolved. Although questions continued to arise in the following weeks, concerns become more serious in July 1991 when Alan D. Fiers, Jr., who had been head of the DDO's Central American Task Force during Iran-contra, pleaded guilty to charges of withholding information from Congress. Fiers also said that then-DDO Clair George knew of the diversion of Iranian funds to the contras. This admission meant that senior officials above and below Gates, both Casey and George, knew about Iran-contra when it was going on, thus renewing questions about Gates, who maintained his previous position. In September 1991, Clair George was indicted on 10 felony counts; George denied his guilt.[130]

With the situation further clouded, the Senate Intelligence Committee delayed consideration of Gates's nomination until the end of the summer. The hearings focused on two major issues, Iran-contra, about which Gates now admitted to misjudgments, and allegations by past and current CIA employees that Gates had "doctored" intelligence to suit his political masters. This aspect of the hearings offered the public its most vivid look at the sometimes hotly contested analytical side of intelligence, far from the cerebral and detached image that some agencies have sought to project. Gates was subjected to the most rigorous hearings of any DCI nominee, but ultimately was confirmed by the Senate and became DCI in November 1991. His hearings yielded for him the curious mandate of "reforming" U.S. intelligence against some fairly vague standard of need, and an admonition by Chairman David Boren that the Senate committee would be watching Gates's performance carefully in light of the allegations raised concerning his management of analysis.

Gates moved swiftly to show that he understood the Senate's mandate. In a December 1991 speech to employees, he called on them to scrap their focus on the cold war and to concentrate on such threats as nuclear proliferation and narcotics. He also spoke of a 15 percent reduction in the CIA over the next several years, largely through attrition, and of changes he planned for the agencies involved in satellite reconnaissance programs.[131] According to press reports, President Bush signed National Security Review 29 (NSR-29), ordering greater intelligence community concentration on such issues as global health problems and natural resources shortages but without dramatic cutbacks in the size of the intelligence community. Rather, current offices and personnel would be transferred or redirected. Interestingly, the Bush directive went to both traditional intelligence community agencies and to such nontraditional agencies as the Environmental Protection Agency, the Department of Health and Human Services, and NASA, reflecting the changed nature of emerging post–cold war intelligence concerns.[132]

As a result of the NSR-29 review, the Commonwealth of Independent States was seen as the greatest concern, given its political and economic instability, potential large sales of excess weapons, and control of nuclear weapons. Other topics of concern included weapons proliferation, narcotics, terrorism, potentially adverse financial and trade issues, and environmental, natural resource, and health issues.[133] Without knowing the details of priorities and resource allocation among these issues, it is difficult to assess the net effect of NSR-29 beyond producing a grab-bag list of so-called new issues to replace the now diminished post-Soviet threat.[134]

As he detailed in April 1992, Gates also took steps to reorganize the intelligence community. He had appointed 14 task forces to review a wide range of issues – openness, politicization, production, collection, et cetera – and began making changes based, in part, on their recommendations. The task force on the politicization of intelligence held that the CIA had not slanted its analysis for policymakers, blaming poor management and the inexperience of some analysts for the growth of the politicization perception. It was also reported that Gates was disturbed over the prevalence of the perception within the CIA.[135]

Efforts at Post-Cold War Reorganization

The Senate and House Intelligence committees were not willing to leave the issue of reorganizing the post-cold war intelligence community entirely up to the executive branch. In 1992, Senator Boren and Representative Dave McCurdy introduced bills giving their visions of potential changes for the intelligence community. The two bills held key points in common; both bills

- created an NSC Committee on Foreign Intelligence to provide overall direction for intelligence
- redesignated the DCI as the director of national intelligence (DNI), with enhanced authority over the entire intelligence community—especially the allocation, obligation, and expenditure of NFIP funds, which would be submitted to Congress as a separate budget
- created a deputy DNI (DDNI) for the intelligence community and a DDNI for Estimates and Analysis
- provided for the CIA to have a separate director subordinate to the DNI, who would be responsible for human collection (HUMINT) and other clandestine collection, and covert actions
- created an Office of Intelligence Analysis, bringing together analysts from throughout the intelligence community
- provided legislative charters for NSA and DIA
- created a National Imagery Agency to unify imagery collection activities and tasking.

As could be expected, some of these concepts, such as the DNI, were not new, and many were controversial. It was also not clear whether the committees expected these bills to pass in some form in the time remaining to the 102nd

Congress or whether, like the original charter legislation in 1976, these were seen as "talking papers" intended to focus debate and fine-tune proposals.

Hearings held by both committees revealed sharply divided opinion among expert witnesses. Many witnesses agreed that this was an appropriate time to examine the intelligence community's structure and role, but broad discussion on which steps to take raised major questions: Should analysis be separated from operations in the CIA? What effect would the Office of Intelligence Analysis have on the idea of "competitive analysis" by separate agencies that, in part, served policymakers with distinct requirements? And what effect would various proposals (DNI control of the NFIP, the National Imagery Agency) have on Defense Department intelligence requirements? Underlying the ensuing debate were three more fundamental questions. First, the bills renewed the issue as to what was the best way to reorganize intelligence: executive orders, which preserved maximum flexibility for the primary intelligence consumer (the president) and his subordinates, or legislation, which would be more permanent. Second, some questioned whether the end of the cold war necessitated a wholesale reorganization of the intelligence community, or if the necessary readjustment to changing events could be accomplished by a reallocation of scaled-back resources. Finally, some questioned whether it was wise to reduce intelligence capabilities at a time of increased global instability when defense capabilities were also being reduced.

Predictably, Secretary of Defense Cheney came out strongly against the bills, arguing that the potential loss of control over certain assets and activities would weaken intelligence support for Defense. In his testimony before a rare joint hearing of the two intelligence committees, DCI Gates first discussed the current state of change at CIA as a result of his task forces. Changes included the following: abolition of the Intelligence Community Staff, which many had seen as a weak link in the DCI's community-wide duties, and its replacement by a DCI Community Management Staff headed by an executive director for community affairs, housed with the DCI at the CIA; reduction in the number of formal DDI publications; greater attention in analysis to alternative scenarios; management and review procedures altered to deal with concerns about politicization (although it was not seen as a pervasive problem), and the appointment of an ombudsman to deal with allegations of politicization; improved internal communication within CIA; and greater efforts toward openness for some CIA products and activities.

Turning to broader community issues, Gates supported the traditional idea of decentralized agencies (as opposed to the Office of Intelligence Analysis), with only the National Intelligence Council acting as a community-wide analytical office, and recommended maximum flexibility. Gates enhanced the NIC's role in overseeing community-wide analysis, including changes to undertake postmortems and to include dissents and alternative scenarios and took steps to improve coordination of HUMINT and open sources. Gates said that one task force also supported a National Imagery Agency, but that such a concept was still under discussion given Defense Department concerns. Gates concluded by saying that given these changes, legislation was unnecessary.

To a certain degree, the debate over the intelligence community had come full circle, back to many of the issues that had surfaced at the end of World War II and at the beginning of the cold war. In the end, no answer was likely to be final, given that intelligence issues and requirements would continue to change.

9

Observations

The collapse of the Soviet satellite empire in 1989 and of the Soviet Union itself in 1991 both resulted in calls for reforming and reducing the U.S. intelligence community. The short interval between these events and the calls for reform and reduction, as well as the underlying assumption – that these changes likely decreased the need for the intelligence community – shows how closely many continued to connect the intelligence community and the cold war. Few raised the equally valid counterargument that in a world of increased uncertainty – of new power balances, greater diffusion of power, increasing weapons proliferation, and political instability in the nuclear-armed former Soviet republics – the need for reliable intelligence has not diminished at all.

Whatever its accomplishments of the past 45 years, the intelligence community must now restate reasons for its existence even as the entire national security policy community attempts to redefine the key issues for the United States. Under these circumstances, the role that the intelligence community plays in this redefinition could be crucial to its future. The community's ability to take part honestly and in a manner that is not seen as self-serving will help ensure more than just reduced survival – not necessarily an easy task as the most foreseeable issues lack the compelling and starkly threatening nature of a nuclear-armed, ideologically proselytizing, united Soviet Union.

The rapid and largely unexpected end of the cold war also raises significant questions about the intelligence community's performance. After more than 40 years of intense analysis, why was the breadth and depth of rot in the Soviet system so badly underestimated? Why did no one even guess the apparently astronomical level of Soviet gross national product devoted to self-debilitating defense, or the effects this would have on the Soviet Union overall? The intelligence community has always been reluctant to undertake postmortems, yet it would seem that a postmortem on the Soviet Union is called for. Not only is there probably much to learn; such introspection would also help assure those bent on reform that the intelligence community is serious about adapting itself to changed circumstances.

Such a process of self-evaluation would not be easy for U.S. intelligence, given its admittedly uneven record, which raises the difficult issue of the community's "batting average" or, as it is more usually phrased, "success versus failure." Here the community runs into a paradox. Although no one realistically expects perfection of the intelligence community, it is not clear what degree of error is permissible or which areas are less important so as to allow flawed analysis. Realistically, no such clarification is possible. Unfortunately, it leaves the intelligence community with a standard of perfection, and with *any* flawed analysis being trumpeted as an "intelligence failure." There is a large difference between flawed analyses or unexpected events (even some major ones) and genuine intelligence failures—that is, mistakes so glaring and of such magnitude that major policies or even national security itself are threatened. Moreover, such a viewpoint places more of the burden than seems fair on the intelligence producers and not enough on the intelligence consumers. The consumers are much more than just passive receivers. They set the agenda of issues and the focus within these issues and can dictate the direction and priorities of intelligence collection – even the content of analysis – depending on how they react to "bad news."[136]

Although the post-cold war period poses significant problems for intelligence analysis, it may prove a boon to intelligence operations. The operations that have tended to become problems, even political disasters, were the open-ended paramilitary operations. It becomes difficult, without the prism of the cold war, to envision many near-term future scenarios that will call for such operations. This does not mean an end to all intelligence operations; there are other types of operations – smaller, better defined – that will still be necessary and that entail less risk for domestic politics. Still, a scaling back of operations may be likely.

Indeed, scaling back may become the *leitmotif* for all U.S. foreign policy. Although the United States is a global power with far-flung interests, the expansion of the cold war from Europe to northeast Asia to the decolonized Third World had also expanded interests in a bipolar struggle. The absence of this struggle may witness a scaling back of U.S. interests as well. This could allow a reduction of U.S. intelligence efforts, but only *after* national interests are redefined and reassessed, not as an opening gesture.

Such a scaling back might also allow U.S. intelligence to step away from the glare of publicity in which it has been held since 1975. There will never be a return to the "good old days" of the cold war in terms of license or the absence of rigorous congressional oversight – nor is that necessary or even desirable. But it may be possible for the analytic community to do its job with greater concentration if it develops some sense that it can work within a proper cloak of classification and without being a highly politicized and partisan shuttlecock. Indeed, many in the intelligence community might see that as a successful trade for reduced size and less compelling foreign policy issues.

II

The Anatomy of U.S. Intelligence

10

Central Coordination and Management

Broadly speaking, the structure of U.S. intelligence has been relatively stable since its inception during the period 1946–1949. The basic concepts worked out then largely survived intact through the collapse of Soviet power in 1991, albeit with necessary modifications and adjustments required by changing needs and relationships. At the time of this writing in early 1992, the House and Senate Intelligence committees were reexamining the role and structure across the board in the community, although it is not clear if these reviews will result in major functional or structural changes. In the following chapters, data on staffing and budgets are drawn from unclassified sources.

Director of Central Intelligence

The position of director of central intelligence predates the creation of the CIA. There has been a DCI since 1946, when President Harry Truman signed a presidential directive creating the Central Intelligence Group, the successor to the wartime Office of Strategic Services. The 1947 National Security Act gave a statutory basis to U.S. intelligence, including the DCI. The DCI is nominated by the president, serving at his pleasure without a set term. The nomination is vetted by the Senate Intelligence Committee (before 1976 by the Senate Armed Services Committee) and is subject to confirmation by the Senate.

The National Security Act is vague on the duties of the DCI, beyond stating that he is the head of the CIA, which itself comes under the National Security Council, and stating the functions of the CIA.[137] Most of the section pertaining to the DCI deals with the limits on his authority and the issue of reimbursement should the DCI be a military officer.

This vagueness has been at the core of the DCI's problems in exercising overall management and coordination of the intelligence community, which is the DCI's supposed role. Initially, the DCI lacked power over the major bureaucratic levers necessary to carry out these duties – budget, resource allocation, and tasking. Several commissions over the years noted these flaws (the Hoover Commission in 1955, the Murphy Commission in 1975, the Rockefeller Commission in 1975) and also remarked on the DCI's administrative burden, which was doubled by the changed role of the CIA. The CIA was originally envisioned as a central unit responsible for advising the NSC on intelligence activities, coordinating these activities, and correlating, evaluating, and disseminating intelligence. Instead, the CIA became an independent collector and producer of intelligence in its own right, as well as the major operational intelligence arm.

Instead of assisting the DCI in his central NSC role, therefore, the CIA provided him with additional intelligence responsibilities. It should be noted, however, that the early DCIs abetted this trend in their early bureaucratic struggles. This change in the CIA also meant that the DCI was no longer a fully independent agent in dealing with other intelligence agencies – especially in analytical disputes – because he sometimes had to defend "his agency" (the CIA) and its products. There is one further problem in this regard. CIA's two main analytic competitors, the DIA and

INR, each report to a cabinet-level customer. The CIA's main customer is the president, which gives the CIA access to the ultimate intelligence consumer but limits its bureaucratic clout; most DCIs will not wish to engage the president in many of their bureaucratic battles.

The DCI did not receive the fuller explicit authority needed to carry out his central role of managing and coordinating national foreign intelligence until the mid-1970s, when a series of public executive orders were issued by successive presidents detailing organization, roles, and permitted activities. Although President Gerald Ford's E.O. 11905 (February 19, 1976) designated the DCI as the president's primary adviser on foreign intelligence, it was President Jimmy Carter's E.O. 12036 (January 28, 1978) that more explicitly spelled out the DCI's authority in the areas of budget, tasking, intelligence review, coordination and dissemination, and foreign liaison.

President Ronald Reagan's E.O. 12333 (December 4, 1981) remains the governing order as of 1992, as President Bush saw no need to supersede it. E.O. 12333 designates the DCI "as the primary adviser to the president and the NSC on national foreign intelligence." The DCI's duties include implementation of special activities (covert action); liaison with foreign intelligence and counterintelligence; protection of intelligence sources, methods, and analytical procedures; "full responsibility for production and dissemination of national foreign intelligence," including the authority to task other intelligence organizations; authority to decide on conflicts in tasking; development of the NFIP budget and implementation and evaluation of the NFIP; and liaison with Congress.

These grants give the DCI more explicit authority than he had before the issuance of the first public executive order in 1976. They also represent a definite improvement in the DCI's authority to carry out his central intelligence community role. Needless to say, this does not mean that interagency disputes over budget, tasking, resources, and the substance of intelligence products are at an end—or that they are all settled amicably. Indeed, it can be argued that in the area of substantive differences over intelligence products, the DCI's authority has most often been debatable even as he has exerted it most forcefully, a reversal of the usual complaint about the weakness of the position. The reason for this lies in the nature of the NIE, which is seen as the "DCI's piece of paper" and goes out over his signature. Two recent DCIs, Stansfield Turner and William Casey, were criticized for making changes in texts to suit their own preferences. Such an action, although the prerogative of the DCI, raises questions. Given that NIEs are supposed to represent the consensus opinion of the community (when such consensus exists), does such action by the DCI undercut this basic premise? Further, some have questioned the reasons for which DCIs made such changes, suggesting that they might be trimming intelligence to suit the known policy preferences of political leaders.

The extent to which DCIs divide their time between their community-wide and CIA responsibilities, or between operations and analysis within the CIA, remains up to the preferences of each incumbent. Such issues are unlikely to be settled with any finality within the current structure. It has often been suggested, most recently in the wake of Iran-contra, that the DCI be separated from the CIA and perhaps renamed the director of national intelligence. Such a step would solve the issue of dual roles, but could further weaken the new DNI by removing him from any bureaucratic support within the intelligence community and perhaps making him even more susceptible to political pressures from policymakers. This issue resurfaced in 1992 when the House and Senate Intelligence committees suggested such a change in legislation, including enhanced DNI authority over the NFIP. As could be expected, the Defense Department objected to any changes that would diminish their control over intelligence resources.

In April 1992, DCI Gates announced a change in how he would manage his community-wide responsibilities. He abolished the Intelligence Community Staff (ICS), replacing it with a DCI Community Management Staff "to strengthen centralized coordination and management." This new staff, headed by an executive director for intelligence community affairs, will be housed at CIA headquarters, unlike the ICS, which was specifically located apart from the CIA to distinguish between the DCI's two roles. The new staff has broad responsibilities for the intelligence community program and budget and will manage overall intelligence requirements to ensure coordination among the major types of collection, as well as to evaluate their performance. The staff will include the position of open source coordinator, who will catalog the entire intelligence community's open source (that is, unclassified) holdings, establish a comprehensive requirements system for acquiring new open sources, improve the sharing of such sources throughout the community, and work with the managers of the other types of intelligence collection to ensure that they do not spend time and resources collecting intelligence that can be obtained openly.

It is too soon to assess the effects of these changes. Many observers believed that the ICS was a weak link in the community that did little to help the DCI exercise his community-wide role. Bringing these functions into closer day-to-day contact with the DCI may help, although locating the staff in CIA headquarters may lead other components in the community to believe that this is simply a CIA office supervising brethren agencies. In fairness, however, much of the DCI's problem stems not from various organizational plans, but from the fact that the secretary of defense has greater direct day-to-day control over the budgets and staffs of more intelligence assets than does the DCI.

The new emphasis on open sources is a significant change. Many in and out of the community have long believed that open sources were too often downplayed simply because they did not have the cachet of imagery, signals, human reporting, et cetera. In a period in which intelligence budgets are likely to shrink, greater reliance on and coordination of open sources may be one way to maintain a necessary flow of information while saving scarce resources for those issues where clandestine collection is absolutely mandatory.

Deputy Director of Central Intelligence

The deputy director of Central Intelligence (also referred to as the deputy DCI or DDCI) has existed de facto since 1947. In 1949 the position received statutory recognition in the Executive Pay Act; full statutory authority came in a 1953 amendment to the National Security Act.

Like the DCI, the deputy DCI's nomination is vetted by the Senate Intelligence Committee and is subject to Senate confirmation. The National Security Act specifies that although either the DCI or the deputy DCI may be an active duty or retired military officer, at no time can both positions be occupied by active duty or retired military officers.

The deputy DCI has full authority to act for the DCI if the latter is absent or disabled and can act to assist the DCI in carrying out those duties vested in him by law. The precise division of responsibilities between the two has largely depended on the preferences of the DCI and those aspects of his job on which he concentrates. This issue became controversial during the two nominations of Robert Gates to be DCI regarding the degree of his knowledge of the Iran-contra affair while he served as Casey's deputy. Gates claimed not to have known of or been involved in Iran-contra until shortly before the scandal broke. Critics wondered how a deputy DCI could credibly make such a claim; others argued that it was possible, given the compartmentalization prevalent in the CIA and Casey's own dominance of operations. The issue reflects both the malleability and limitations of the deputy DCI position.

National Foreign Intelligence Board

The National Foreign Intelligence Board is the most recent in a series of several intelligence community management boards designed to assist the DCI in carrying out his community role. The NFIB was first publicly recognized in President Carter's E.O. 12036 in 1978, with responsibility for advising the DCI on intelligence production, review, and coordination, the intelligence budget, and other matters.

Under the Reagan administration, the NFIB was restructured to deal with analytical and substantive issues, advising the DCI on the collection, processing, production, review, and coordination of intelligence; on the protection of sources and methods; and on foreign liaison. NIEs come before the NFIB for final approval, including working out interagency disagreements that cannot be resolved by the drafters.

The DCI chairs the NFIB. Other members are the deputy DCI, who is both vice chairman and the CIA representative;[138] the directors of the Defense Intelligence Agency and the National Security Agency; the assistant secretary of state for intelligence and research; the assistant director of the FBI (Intelligence Division); the assistant secretary of energy for defense programs; and the special assistant to the secretary of the treasury (national security). Representatives of the intelligence units of the military services and the Defense Department's specialized intelligence offices attend as observers. Other agencies may attend, depending on the topic or issue under discussion. NFIB meetings tend to be limited to principals only.

National Foreign Intelligence Council

The National Foreign Intelligence Council (NFIC) evolved out of the NFIB's restructuring during the Reagan administration. The NFIC makes resource allocations within the

NFIP and sets NFIP priorities, concentrating more on management than on analytical or operational issues. The DCI chairs the NFIC; the deputy DCI is vice chairman and the CIA representative, or, as in NFIB, is replaced by the DDI as the CIA representative when the deputy DCI is in the chair. NFIC membership parallels that of the NFIB but also includes the military services, Defense Department specialized reconnaissance offices, and senior representatives of the secretary of defense, the attorney general, the secretary of commerce, and the assistant to the president for national security affairs. In 1992, DCI Gates named the chairman of the National Intelligence Council to be an NFIC member as part of his general upgrading of the NIC as the "sole Community analytical structure." Unlike the NFIB, NFIC meetings are not necessarily limited to principals.

National Security Council

The NSC is not usually considered to be a part of the intelligence community – a key point in the Iran-contra affair – but is central to the functions of the DCI and CIA. Created by the National Security Act of 1947, the NSC serves to "advise the President with respect to the integration of domestic, foreign and military policies relating to the national security," thereby enhancing interdepartmental efforts in the national security area. Before the NSC, this necessary integrative function was either carried out informally or by a series of somewhat limited bodies, including the Standing Liaison Committee (1938–1943), which brought together the departments of State, War, and Navy, and the State-War-Navy Coordinating Committee (1945–1949). The demands of a global war and postwar uncertainties in foreign affairs revealed a need for some forum to integrate the various aspects of defense, foreign, and domestic policy, and thus the NSC was formed.

The DCI serves under the NSC, as does the CIA, although the DCI is not a statutory member of the NSC.

Statutory members are the president, vice president, and the secretaries of state and defense. The DCI attends as the NSC's intelligence adviser; the chairman of the Joint Chiefs of Staff advises on military matters. The assistant to the president for national security affairs also attends. This position is customarily for managing the day-to-day activities of the NSC staff; it is not subject to confirmation by the Senate.

The organization of the NSC staff is not prescribed by law; each president has used it to suit his own personal working methods, including the control and oversight of intelligence.[139] Under President Truman there was an Interdepartmental Intelligence Conference. The Eisenhower NSC staff included the U.S. Intelligence Board – a predecessor of the NFIB – and the Interdepartmental Intelligence Conference. Presidents Kennedy and Johnson had very rudimentary NSC structures. During the Carter administration, broad policy and managerial issues came under the Policy Review Board; the Special Coordination Committee handled operational intelligence issues.

The most detailed NSC staff apparatus in general, and certainly with respect to intelligence, existed under Presidents Nixon and Ford. The NSC staff included the Intelligence Committee; the Verification Panel (devoted to the verification aspect of SALT); the "40" Committee (for covert action); and the Intelligence Resources Advisory Committee (IRAC). Except for IRAC, all of those committees were chaired by Henry Kissinger, the assistant to the president for national security affairs. Indeed, one of the criticisms of the NSC staff during this period was that it was overly dominated by Kissinger. This criticism continued even after Kissinger relinquished his NSC post in 1975 while continuing to serve as secretary of state – and after President Ford restructured the NSC staff as part of his overall intelligence reorganization in February 1976.[140]

The tremendous growth in power of the assistant to the president for national security affairs was an unforeseen outgrowth of the NSC structure, beginning with the role of

McGeorge Bundy under President Kennedy. The rivalry for primacy in U.S. foreign policy that resulted between the national security adviser (as the position is popularly known) and the secretary of state (Bundy vs. Rusk, Kissinger vs. Rogers, Brzezinski vs. Vance) was the most frequently cited issue concerning the overall role played by the NSC staff – that is, until the Reagan administration.

The Reagan administration was an unsettling period for the NSC staff. First, there were six national security advisers over the eight years, representing a fairly wide range of interests, talents, and expertise.[141] Second, as illustrated in the Iran-contra affair, there is a very fine line between policy coordination and policy advocacy. Even before members of the NSC staff got involved in what were essentially covert actions, the staff was generating papers advocating policies (a potential opening to Iran) on its own that did not reflect any sentiment in the traditional policy bureaucracies – State and Defense. The behavior of the NSC staff in this instance is not easily assessed, as there will inevitably be instances in which the preferences of the president, to which the NSC staff responds most readily, will thwart preferences of the departments, which may even serve to quash preferred policies.

A third issue arising from the Reagan years was the propriety of the NSC staff's engaging in intelligence operations, including the creating of its own "off the shelf" logistics capability to support paramilitary operations. Unlike the preparation of policy papers, this activity represented a serious change in normal procedures, both within the executive and in relations with Congress. The terms of the oversight provisions worked out in 1991 make it less likely for such an operational role to recur without the knowledge of Congress.

For the fiscal year ending September 30, 1991, the NSC staff had 57 full-time employees, with a requested budget of $5.893 million. These figures do not necessarily include staff members detailed from other agencies.

Office of Management and Budget

The intelligence budget is handled by the Office of Management and Budget's Intelligence Branch of the National Security Division. The branch has a staff of six. (The budgets of the military services' intelligence units are separate and handled as part of the larger military budget.) As with all other budget requests, the Intelligence Branch receives the requests of the agencies, in this case the National Foreign Intelligence Program prepared by the DCI and NFIC. OMB then reviews and evaluates the request and gives the president a final recommendation to include in his budget presentation to Congress. Agencies may appeal OMB decisions; the president is the final adjudicator.

OMB's handling of the intelligence budget has come under criticism. In its 1980 annual report, the House Intelligence Committee found that OMB was "rearranging" priorities set by the DCI, setting "sometimes inflexible ceilings," and that its recommendations on the NFIP "sometimes are seriously flawed." The committee noted that it had to act either to preserve currently needed capabilities or to develop new ones, which required higher priorities than projects favored by OMB.[142] Such a situation, although not unique to intelligence, may be a special problem in an area depending on expensive and highly sophisticated technology that is, in general, arcane even to many in the intelligence community itself.

11

Intelligence Agencies and Components

Bureau of Intelligence and Research

The Bureau of Intelligence and Research (INR) is the State Department's own producer, disseminator, and coordinator of intelligence and also serves as the main point of contact between the State Department and the rest of the intelligence community. The idea of having separate, dedicated intelligence producers to meet the specific and, at some level, unique needs of major policymakers (INR for State; DIA for Defense; CIA for the president), is important, as it is one of two major reasons for what many see as redundancy in the intelligence community. The other reason is the idea of competitive analysis – that is, when many groups of analysts with differing points of view work on an issue, they can perhaps come closer to what is actually going on.

Of the three agencies that produce all-source finished intelligence (CIA, DIA, and INR), INR is unique because it has no dedicated intelligence collectors of its own, although it does have daily access to all of the sources available to the other agencies. INR's structure and role was long an issue, with the bureau divided between two groups: those advocating a close relationship with policymakers so as to contribute to and perhaps influence decisions and those advocating some distance so as to free intelligence from policy demands and the chance of being subjective about certain issues. The debate is not unique to INR, although nowhere else in the intelligence community did it rage with such prolonged intensity. Since the directorship of Roger Hilsman in the early 1960s, INR has been oriented toward a close relationship with policymakers, following the general trend throughout the community.

INR is headed by an assistant secretary, who is subject to confirmation by the Senate. (Before the mid-1980s, the head of INR was called the director and was not subject to Senate confirmation.) Two deputy assistant secretaries are responsible for the day-to-day production of intelligence analysis. Under functional analysis are the offices for Economics; Geography (headed by the geographer of the United States); Political-Military; Strategic and Proliferation; and Terrorism and Narcotics. Under regional analysis are six offices covering the various regions of the globe. There is also a deputy assistant secretary for coordination, who handles INR and State's liaison with operational elements in the intelligence community.

Since the Wriston reforms of the 1950s, INR has been staffed by a mixture of foreign service officers (roughly 40 percent) and civil servants (roughly 60 percent). With this mixture, INR combines analysts who can develop long-term expertise (civil servants) with analysts who have first-hand knowledge of their regions or policy issues and have been and will be intelligence consumers as well.

The principal INR product is the "Secretary's Morning Summary" (known in-house as "the Book"), comprising a series of short gists and analyses of current intelligence and some longer analyses of larger scope or focus. The secretary and his senior subordinates as well as other intelligence agencies and major policy offices receive this each morning. It is the principal rival to the CIA's "National Intelligence Daily." In addition, each INR office puts out one or two "magazines" on a weekly or biweekly basis covering the breadth of issues on which it works. Like all other State bureaus, INR also sends memos directly to the secretary and contributes to NIEs and other intelligence community products.

In 1991, INR had 361 employees and a budget of approximately $24 million. Its size, which has been relatively stable since a large reduction in the 1960s, is one of the issues INR faces. As one of the largest bureaus within State, its size is harder to increase and easier to cut. Yet within the intelligence community, INR is much smaller than either the CIA or DIA. Compensating for this mismatch in size are two INR advantages: first, its location in the same building as its major policy customers; second, its smaller size, compared with the CIA and DIA, which means fewer bureaucratic and managerial layers and more responsiveness on occasion than the more ponderous bureaucracies of its rivals.

Another problem for INR is its inability to recruit from among the best FSOs. Intelligence work is not recognized as a major requirement for a successful career. Indeed, many FSOs believe that a tour in INR can harm career prospects, although there is no evidence to support this negative legend.

Finally, the relative importance of INR within State has waxed and waned over the years. As a functional bureau, it is viewed as somewhat less central to State's day-to-day mission, compared with the various regional bureaus that control U.S. embassies in their regions and contribute to policies in Washington. (The same problem is true of the Bureau of Politico-Military Affairs.) The functional bureaus depend—perhaps more than the regional bureaus—on the bureaucratic savvy and clout of their assistant secretaries and on their access to the secretary, based to a large degree on how the secretary manages the department overall.

Central Intelligence Agency

The CIA was established by the National Security Act of 1947, under the National Security Council. Its stated function in the act is to coordinate "the intelligence activities of the several Government departments and agencies in the interest of national security." To carry out this function, the CIA was specifically designated to

- advise the NSC on government intelligence activities related to national security
- make recommendations to the NSC on coordinating intelligence activities
- coordinate, evaluate, and disseminate intelligence, with a specific proviso against any "police, subpoena, law-enforcement powers, or internal security functions," and with no exclusive role in collection, evaluation, or dissemination
- perform "additional services of common concern" as directed by the NSC for efficient central management
- perform "such other functions and duties related to intelligence" as directed by the NSC.

The original concept, as conceived by President Truman, was that the CIA would be a central management and coordination unit. Instead, it became one of three (along with the DIA and INR) producers of all-source finished intelligence and an operational unit. Many of the central management functions are handled by the new DCI Community Management Staff, not by the CIA.

The CIA has four major divisions: the Directorate for Administration (DDA), the Directorate for Intelligence (DDI), the Directorate for Operations (DDO), and the Directorate for Science and Technology (DDS&T). The DDA is responsible for administration and management functions, including personnel, budget, security, medical services, and overseas logistical support.

The DDI, the largest of the CIA's directorates, is the main producer of intelligence. Created in 1952, the DDI is responsible for both the production of finished intelligence and for overt collection. (During the Carter administration, the DDI was renamed the National Foreign Assessment Center or NFAC; DCI Casey later reinstated its earlier name.)

The deputy director for intelligence (known, as is his organization, as the DDI), oversees four specific functional staffs: Arms Control Intelligence, Collections Requirements and Evaluation, Planning and Management, and Product Evaluation. He also oversees the offices of Current Production, Global Issues, Imagery Analysis, Information Resources, Leadership Analysis, and Scientific and Weapons Research, as well as five regional offices.

The DDO, the operational branch of the CIA, is responsible for clandestine collection, counterintelligence, and covert operations. Although it is probably the most well-known part of the CIA, at least in terms of popular image, the DDO actually represents a relatively small share of personnel and resources.

The DDS&T is responsible for basic and applied scientific research and development, the design and operation of technical collection systems, and the production of finished scientific and technical intelligence. Its offices include Research and Development, Research and Engineering, the Foreign Broadcast Information Service or FBIS (which monitors and reports on media broadcasts worldwide), SIGINT (signals intelligence) Operations, Technical Service, and the National Photographic Interpretation Center.

There are also a number of offices that report to the DCI, including the General Counsel, and the recently created Inspector General.

Unlike the DIA and INR, the CIA does not have a major day-to-day departmental client. Rather, it is viewed as "the President's intelligence agency." Although this direct access offers special opportunities, it also can undercut CIA effectiveness; it has no policy companions or superiors who may be more available than the president and more interested in supporting what may be parochial CIA interests.

This position also means that the CIA is caught between its role as an intelligence producer and its supposed role as an intelligence coordinator. It is patently difficult for the CIA to coordinate objectively when it is also presenting its view of an issue, a problem that sometimes has surfaced in the drafting of NIEs. The general effectiveness of the CIA in its central role is greatly affected by how the DCI chooses to carry out his dual role.

The major CIA contribution to current intelligence is the "National Intelligence Daily" or NID (actually a misnomer, because it is not produced on Sundays). It is structured much like INR's "Morning Summary," with shorter gist/analysis items up front, followed by a few longer, more in-depth pieces. The NID goes out to senior policy and intelligence officials throughout the Washington, D.C., area.

One issue raised about the CIA is whether the operational and analytical branches should be housed under the same roof. Those who argue for separation of the branches believe that the presence of operations tends to warp the focus of analysis, making it less objective on issues where operations may be an ongoing factor. Defenders of the current arrangement maintain that the two branches benefit from proximity; the operators (in this case, clandestine collectors) gain a better sense of what the analysts require, and the analysts acquire some sense of the world beyond their office walls. The bills introduced by the House and Senate Intelligence Committees in 1992 would separate the two.

The size of the CIA and the career management of its analysts are also at issue. Some argue that the CIA's size and its many layers of management and review have grown ponderous, slowing down the analytical process and adversely affecting its quality with too many reviewers. The CIA's goal of creating "intelligence generalists" by rotating analysts every few years from one area to another, often seemingly unrelated, area also raises questions. Although this practice avoids the trap – not uncommon among intelligence analysts – of getting caught in an intellectual rut, it runs counter to the desire and necessity of creating bases of long-term expertise on issues; it also risks having analysts perennially study new areas only to leave just as they are beginning to master them.

The Gulf War raised issues anew about the role of human intelligence, its utility as a national intelligence asset, and the CIA management of other national assets. The Senate Intelligence Committee believed that the war reaffirmed the value of human intelligence and revealed the short shrift given to Defense Department HUMINT needs. The committee proposed creating a new assistant DDO (ADDO), who would be a flag rank officer and would represent the Defense Department within the DDO. It also recommended that the deputy director of NPIC alternate every three years between CIA and Defense.

In April 1992, DCI Gates described a number of changes he had made in CIA organization and process. These changes were, in part, a response to the Senate Intelligence Committee's mandate at Gates's confirmation hearings that he review the workings of the intelligence community in the aftermath of the cold war. Gates created 14 task forces, 7 of which focused on CIA issues. These changes were also seen as an effort by the Bush administration to control the process of intelligence reorganization in the face of legislation being proposed by the House and Senate Intelligence committees.

Gates said the DDI would reduce the number of formal publications it issued and would give components greater autonomy to respond directly to requests from policy agencies. Addressing the issues of layering and review, Gates said that practices in those areas would be reviewed, and the DDI himself would only review sensitive products intended for the highest-level policy consumers. Finally, reflecting criticisms directed against him about politicizing intelligence, as well as a task force report showing concern throughout the CIA, Gates noted that analyses would include more alternative views and appointed an ombudsman to act as an independent and informal counselor for those who had complaints in this area. The inspector general would also be active in this area.

In the DDO, Gates announced that an ADDO for military affairs had been created, held by a flag rank military officer. There is also an Office for Military Affairs to improve CIA support to military planning, exercises, and operations. A National Human Tasking Center has been created to coordinate HUMINT tasking requirements; this center includes representatives from Defense and INR.

Defense Intelligence Agency

The DIA was founded in 1961 as part of Secretary of Defense Robert McNamara's efforts to rationalize the Defense Department's organization, to unify Defense Department intelligence efforts, and to improve the management and utilization of the department's resources for intelligence collection, production, and dissemination.

The DIA serves as the principal foreign military intelligence arm of the secretary of defense, the JCS, the Unified and Specified Military Commands, and other Defense Department components. It may also serve agencies that are not part of the Defense Department. The DIA is responsible for providing military intelligence for national foreign intelligence products, coordinating Defense Department intelligence collection requirements, managing and operating the Defense Attaché System, and providing foreign intelligence and counterintelligence support to the JCS.

The agency is headed by a military officer of three-star rank, a position that customarily rotates among the services. The director of the DIA is subject to confirmation by the Senate; his nomination is vetted by the Senate Armed Services Committee. As the DIA is a joint military agency, its personnel are drawn from each of the services; there are also many civilian analysts and managers in the DIA.

Of the major intelligence components, the DIA was the first to feel the effects of the post–cold war period. In 1990, Congress mandated a 5 percent annual cut in DIA personnel over each of the next five years, despite the objections of the House Intelligence Committee. In 1991, the DIA became the subject of a tug of war between the assistant secretary of defense for command, control, and communications, Duane Andrews, and the Congress. The Senate Armed Services Committee objected to a March 1991 defense reorganization that gave Andrews much greater control over the DIA and its General Defense Intelligence Program or GDIP—that is, its budget. The Defense Department held that the change would improve priority setting and general oversight; the Senate Armed Services Committee, however, believed it would politicize the DIA and wrote a one-year charter for the agency to ensure its independence.

At the same time, the DIA underwent a major reorganization, resulting in the following structure:

The Directorate for Current Intelligence, Joint Staff and Command Support (J2), concentrates on near-term intelligence issues and operational support. It comprises the following offices: Counterdrug Support; Unified and Specified Command and Joint Staff Support; Current Intelligence; Organizational Readiness; and Indications and Warning.

The Directorate for Foreign Intelligence is responsible for long-term research, analysis, and estimates and comprises these offices: Scientific and Technical Intelligence, Research and Assessments, and Global Analysis. Global Analysis, although part of Foreign Intelligence, does have some operational support functions for certain issues, runs the Operational Intelligence Crisis Center, and produces counterintelligence analysis. It is expected that Global Analysis will be coordinating much of its work with the Office for Current Intelligence in the other analytical directorate.

There are also directorates for Attachés and Operations; Collection and Imagery Activities; Information Services; and Planning and Administration, which includes the Office for Security and Counterintelligence and in this case means defensive programs rather than analysis. Nine Defense Intelligence Officers (DIOs), counterparts to the NIOs, report to the director of DIA, as does the commandant of the Defense Intelligence College and the Military Intelligence Board (MIB), which is composed of the service intelligence components.

The primary intelligence issue concerning the DIA is the question of its ultimate effectiveness within its parent organization. For the DIA, this issue received renewed and even glaring attention in the aftermath of the Persian Gulf War. In their postwar critiques of overall performance in the Gulf War, the Defense Department and General Schwarzkopf noted shortcomings in support to the theater commander from national intelligence components and assets.[143] Heavily hedged assessments of bomb damage were a particular problem, as was quick access to available imagery.

The DIA's performance problems are compounded by the fact that, within the Defense Department, it serves two masters: the military, represented by the Joint Chiefs, and the civilian leadership, represented by the Office of the Secretary of Defense. Despite their equal devotion to the Defense Department's mission, these two groups do not always see eye-to-eye on such key issues as budget, weapons choices, resource allocation, and arms control. Such differences can pull the DIA between its two masters. DIA's relationship with these two groups also varies. There have been periods in which the leadership of the Office of the Secretary of Defense has been suspicious of the quality and objectivity of military analyses; ironically, McNamara, the creator of DIA, was one such consumer. Conversely, as a military organization staffed and supervised by military personnel, the DIA can be forced to be subjective by the JCS, given the normal process of chain of command.

Another problem for the DIA is its stature within the military. Although intelligence is a recognized career specialty in the military (unlike the Foreign Service), traditionally it has not been seen as a major path for career advancement. Although service in some intelligence capacity may be necessary for a well-rounded career (called "ticket punching"), the main path to promotion has generally been in command positions related to combat readiness and effectiveness.[144] This factor is undoubtedly not as significant as it was before World War II, yet it still has some effect, with some critics maintaining that the DIA–like INR and the FSOs–does not attract the best available officers. A similar criticism has been made of the entire Joint Staff structure that supports the JCS, of which the DIA is a part. Critics argue that most officers consider the best career opportunities those within their own service and that each service wants to keep its best officers for its own exclusive needs.[145]

Although the DIA is one of three all-source producers of finished intelligence (along with the CIA and INR), some question how well it performs that function. The DIA's daily publication, the "Defense Intelligence Summary" (DINSUM), is not viewed by many as on a par with the CIA's NID or INR's "Morning Summary," often giving information that appears better suited for a lower-level audience. Critics charge that, although the DIA has significant and worthwhile capabilities within its sphere, such as details of enemy weaponry and enemy order of battle and strength (sometimes derogatorily called "bean counting"), the agency is out of its depth on broader intelligence issues. Some also question the nature of the DIA's estimates or contribution to NIEs, as these tend to range on the high side–or "worst case"–of any threat. Such a preference is understandable, however, when one takes into account the fact that military planners, one of the DIA's main customers, need to start at such a base to have available the necessary forces to deal with any level of conceivable threat. Still, some argue that this planning necessity carries over into most DIA analyses. It is not clear what effect the mandated five-year reduction in the DIA will have on these problems: Will a streamlined DIA concentrate more of its resources on its strengths, or will this further reduce the agency's ability to fulfill its national intelligence role?

Finally, there is the effect of the DIA's central efforts on the individual military intelligence services. The two programs obviously must compete for the same staff and resources, and some argue that the DIA has undercut the individual programs. Defenders of these separate programs continue to support them, but it remains an area of conflict and internal competition.

Defense Specialized Intelligence Offices

There are a number of offices within the Defense Department that carry out special reconnaissance programs, including photographic, signal, and electronic intelligence. Although the existence of these offices is officially recognized (they are named in E.O. 12333, for example), their precise titles and functions remain classified and do not appear in public official documents.[146]

Among the most important of these is the National Reconnaissance Office (NRO), a part of U.S. Air Force Intelligence. It was reportedly formed in 1960 as a means of coordinating the nascent field of space-borne reconnaissance.[147] The NRO is usually under the direction of the under secretary of the air force for space systems, or the assistant secretary for research and development.[148] NRO's budget is highly classified and would be difficult to discern, given the reported compartmentalization of the intelligence budget in which related projects are not necessarily kept within the budget of one agency or office. At the outset of the Reagan administration, the NRO budget was estimated to be around $2 billion annually. Since then, the figure has likely gone up, given the effects of inflation and the Boren-Cohen initiative mandating additional satellites that was part of the debate over the INF treaty. Although the NRO is responsible for the operation of some of the most expensive systems that the United States buys, there have been reports of very large cost overruns (some at 100 percent or more over budget) resulting from poor management.[149] The management of the NRO typifies the burden of highly complex, costly, and necessarily secret methods versus the need for some external accountability and necessary congressional oversight. Budget control is admittedly difficult when working with frontier technology, just as oversight is difficult given the highly complex nature of the systems involved.

Federal Bureau of Investigation

The main intelligence function of the FBI is counterintelligence. Although other agencies, including the CIA and DIA, have counterintelligence responsibilities of their own, the FBI remains the paramount agency in this field.

The FBI's line of authority goes from the attorney general, who is head of the parent agency, the Department of Justice, to the director of the FBI and, for counterintelligence, to the assistant director in charge of the Intelligence Division. The internal organization, budget, and staffing of the Intelligence Division are classified. The FBI also shares with the CIA responsibility for combating foreign terrorist activities. This work is handled by the Criminal Division, owing to an administrative decision that these cases are more likely to end up in criminal prosecutions. Many espionage cases involve foreign nationals with diplomatic credentials who are immune from prosecution and are deported instead.

E.O. 12333 confirms this major focus of the FBI and also gives the FBI the additional task of coordinating all counterintelligence activities of other agencies conducted within the United States. Those conducted abroad are coordinated by the CIA. The executive order also authorizes the FBI to collect foreign intelligence within the United States or to support foreign intelligence collection requirements and communications security activities.

The ability of the FBI to cope with foreign intelligence activities has long been an issue, albeit one that has recently undergone several changes. The major focus had long been activities by Soviet and Soviet-bloc diplomats posted to the United States, both in Washington and at the United Nations in New York. Not only the FBI but many in Congress believed that the FBI was woefully understaffed for the potential counterintelligence threat, which then-FBI Director William Webster estimated was some 35 percent of the diplomatic missions from "unfriendly" nations.[150]

The so-called Year of the Spy (1985) served to focus renewed attention on the counterintelligence problem, revealing numerous management issues that helped contribute to some of these lapses. Two glaring problems for the FBI were the arrest and conviction of FBI agent Richard Miller for espionage and the FBI's failed surveillance of spy suspect Edward Howard, who managed to escape undetected and eventually turned up in the Soviet Union.

The political transformation of Eastern Europe and what had been the Soviet Union initially complicated the counterintelligence problem. On the one hand, a great deal of information has become available in former Soviet satellites detailing the nature and extent of their relationships with the Soviet Union's KGB and GRU. On the other hand, it was not entirely clear how completely these ties were severed, not in an institutional sense, but in terms of individuals or organizations in Eastern Europe (or at posts abroad) who might still be responding to Russian control or tasking. Nor was it clear to what extent Russia or other former Soviet republics would continue their former intelligence activities despite ongoing political changes, which have included some reorganization of the KGB. The political changes in Eastern Europe and the Soviet Union complicated the FBI's task, however; it could no longer operate on the assumption that all diplomats from these countries were potentially hostile.

By early 1992, when the Soviet Union had ceased to exist as a political entity, the FBI leadership evidently believed that their counterintelligence problems had eased. Attorney General William P. Barr announced that 300 FBI counterintelligence agents (an estimated 12 percent of the counterintelligence strength) were being reassigned to deal with street gangs and violent crime.[151]

The other major change to affect FBI counterintelligence has been the recent spate of U.S.-Soviet arms control agreements (the INF, Threshold Test Ban, and START treaties) that include provisions for on-site inspections – that is, the presence of Soviet or Russian inspectors at sensitive U.S. facilities. This has had two major effects. For the first time, the FBI is now an active participant in U.S. arms control policy deliberations, but in a role that can put it in conflict with other intelligence components. In considering possible provisions for on-site inspections, policy and intelligence agencies concerned with monitoring treaty provisions want as much access to Soviet (or successor republic) facilities as possible, consonant with U.S. security requirements for reciprocal foreign inspections of U.S. facilities. The FBI, on the other hand, tends to want to reduce on-site access, largely in response to its expanded counterintelligence problems.

This second major effect of arms control – that is, the even greater strain on FBI counterintelligence resources – is an area that Congress has flagged for attention and for which it has recommended additional resources.

Military Services

In addition to the joint intelligence effort organized by the DIA, each of the four military services has its own intelligence unit, responding to specific intelligence requirements.[152] To a certain degree, these intelligence units resemble each other in organization and general functions, as would be expected. Each also has specific offices related to its own specific military missions, and each is a member of the NFIC, which deals with intelligence community management and budget issues.

Air Force Intelligence is the largest of the military service intelligence units, in part because it is responsible for the operation of a great many of the U.S. technical collection systems. The main air force intelligence component is the Air Force Intelligence Agency (AFIA), which houses the major analytical functions: Assessments; Studies and Negotiations Support; Threat and Technology; Warning and Regional Assessments. AFIA also oversees air attachés and the Air Force Special Activities Center, which is the air force's human intelligence program. There is a separate Directorate of Policy, Plans, and Programs that oversees logistical and planning functions. Finally, there is the Foreign Technology Division (FTD), a large scientific and technical center concentrating on foreign aircraft and missiles and serving both the air force and the broader intelligence community.

Army intelligence has six major directorates: Foreign Liaison; Foreign Intelligence, the main analytical group, which comprises Current Intelligence, Intelligence Estimates, and Threat Intelligence Development; Intelligence Policy and Operations, which deals with various collection issues; Intelligence Plans and Integration; Counterintelligence and Security Countermeasures; and Intelligence Automation Management.

The Office of Naval Intelligence has a somewhat complex structure. The director has a number of assistants for specific issues: counterintelligence, foreign liaison, counternarcotics, technology, and intelligence community affairs. The Intelligence Division has a senior sovietologist and two junior Soviet analysts and also handles special projects. The Intelligence Analysis Division has four regional offices, a Regional Intelligence Branch, and analytical offices for Military Systems, Submarines, and Surface. There is also a Current Intelligence Division and an Operational Support Division. The Naval Intelligence Operations Group handles navy intelligence collection requirements; the Naval Security Group has cryptographic responsibilities.

The adamancy of the services in maintaining separate intelligence units even after the DIA was formed and began to function has long been an issue. Concerns about overlap and duplication have increased with the burgeoning of intelligence units attached to the various Unified and Specified Commands. The end of the cold war has focused Congress's attention on this issue, making the overall defense intelligence establishment the first to be subjected to reductions and mandates to streamline operations. The Persian Gulf War also raised questions about the value of this redundancy and especially about the ability of the overall apparatus to act as an integrated whole and to supply battlefield commanders with useful, timely intelligence. Critiques of intelligence performance have suggested problems in tactical intelligence and gaps between this level of intelligence and national intelligence. A longer-term issue is the problem of personnel, which also affects the DIA–namely, whether intelligence attracts and promotes the best available people.

National Intelligence Council

Created in 1979, the National Intelligence Council is made up of the National Intelligence Officers (NIOs) under the system initiated by DCI Colby when he abolished the Board of National Estimates. The NIC reports to the DCI. As the home base of the NIOs, the NIC has been most active in preparing NIEs.

In April 1992, DCI Gates announced a significant restructuring of the NIC and an upgrading of its responsibilities. The NIC has a chairman, who has been made a voting member of the NFIC. A new vice chairman for evaluation is responsible for postmortems on previous estimates, assessing the quality and accuracy of analyses, and working with NIOs to identify gaps in critical intelligence, which will then be used to create new collection priorities. There is also a new vice chairman for estimates, who is responsible for managing the NIE production program, making sure that draft estimates include dissents and alternative scenarios, promoting the use of Team A-Team B competitive analyses, and ensuring that draft estimates make clear what is known rather than what is being estimated and reflect the levels of confidence in judgments.[153]

Gates termed the NIC the "sole Community analytical structure," distinguishing it from the CIA, DIA, and INR. This may also have been in reaction to the Senate and House Intelligence committee proposals to create a community-wide Office of Intelligence Analysis. To help the NIC carry out its role, its staff will be increased so that NIEs can be drafted within the NIC staff, rather than having NIOs search for drafters from among the various agencies – usually from CIA, as has been the past practice. Also, the NIC will be moved out of CIA, where it has long been housed, to "an independent facility." Various bodies that formerly reported to the DDI will now report to the NIC instead. These include the National Intelligence Production Board (formerly the Intelligence Producers Council) and a number of specialized community-wide intelligence production committees: the Joint Atomic Energy Intelligence Committee, the Weapons and Space Systems Intelligence Committee, and the Science and Technology Committee.

Finally, according to Gates, the NIC will make greater use of outside experts and scholars in its work, including the person chosen as vice chairman of estimates, a throwback to the earliest days of the Board of National Estimates, which sometimes relied on outside scholars.

It is too soon to assess the effects of this enhanced role of the NIC. Moving the NIC out of the CIA will be psychologically important for the other agencies participating in the NIE process, who have long regarded the NIC as an adjunct of the CIA rather than an independent senior body. Whether the NIC can achieve this independence depends on more than its physical location; an ability to draw on its own staff for NIE drafts rather than on CIA analysts is also important. Critics of past analyses will probably applaud the greater use of postmortems and competitive analysis, both of which were rarely emphasized in the past.

More fundamental questions surround the future of the NIEs themselves. NIEs have been subject to contentious debate, both with regard to their content and to their overall usefulness to decision makers. Problems of length, style (readability), and timeliness have been cited as factors that undercut some NIEs. Special NIEs (SNIEs) are sometimes used for fast-moving events or issues. Some critics have suggested that NIEs serve more to put the entire intelligence community on record about an issue than to help policymakers reach informed decisions. There are also questions as to whether products with such limited use are worth the investment of time and staff they require.[154] Some argue that intelligence agencies participate in NIEs largely because they exist, simply to present and protect their points of view, not because of an inherent belief in their usefulness.

National Security Agency

The NSA remains one of the most secret of the publicly acknowledged intelligence agencies. It was created by a secret presidential directive in 1952; parts of that directive were only recently declassified.

The director of NSA (referred to internally as DIRNSA) is a three-star military officer; the position rotates among the services and is subject to confirmation by the Senate. The NSA comes under the general direction of the secretary of defense, but it is not considered part of the joint defense apparatus as is the DIA. The NSA is an intelligence collector, not a producer of finished intelligence analysis; it is subject to collection requirements from other intelligence community components. Its functions come under the general category of "signals intelligence activities," for which the NSA has primary responsibility according to E.O. 12333. This involves two major roles: the interception and decoding of foreign coded information and the maintenance of the security of U.S. codes.

Estimates of the numbers of NSA personnel range from 80,000 to 120,000, including those assigned overseas. Its budget has been estimated at over $1 billion. By these combined indices, the NSA is presumably the largest of the intelligence components. Much of the NSA budget goes to highly sophisticated computers that are central to its task of decoding intercepted signals.

The organization of the NSA remains classified. James Bamford, in *The Puzzle Palace*, suggests the following internal structure:[155] the main unit is the Office of Signals Intelligence Operations, also known as the DDO. It is responsible for the operational aspects of signals intelligence, including cryptanalysis, traffic analysis of all sorts, and analysis of the cryptanalytical systems of all nations, including those friendly to or allied with the United States. Within the DDO there are three operational groups: A Group, which is responsible for the former Soviet Union and its allies; B Group, which deals with communist nations in Asia; and G Group, which deals with the Third World and all other nations, as well as international telecommunications to and from the United States. In addition, C Group provides computer support, and W Group manages all intercept operations. A number of staff components in the DDO have responsibilities for consumer liaison and the formulation of operational plans and policies. The NSA also runs the National Cryptologic School.

The Office of Communications Security (COMSEC or the S Organization) is responsible for the protection of all U.S. classified communications. Policy for S Organization is made by the U.S. Communications Security Board (comprising the secretaries of defense, state, commerce, and treasury, the attorney general, and the assistant secretary of defense for communication, command, control, and intelligence [C^3I]). According to Bamford, issues unresolved by the board are referred to the secretaries of state and defense, or, if necessary, to the president, although Bamford says this has rarely happened.

Given the central role of advanced computer technology in the NSA's work, the agency has long been interested in the effects of increased numbers of private computers, codes (as used by some financial institutions), private research in cryptology, and computer security. Some of the NSA's concerns have run athwart competing concerns about the free flow of information now being stored in private data bases. In 1978 Congress raised questions about the NSA's role in the National Bureau of Standards' development of a Data Encryption Standard (a uniform method of enciphering non-national security government and non-government data); in 1981, the American Council on Education acceded to an NSA request and formed the Public Cryptology Study Group, to which relevant papers on cryptology would be submitted. In 1984, President Reagan signed National Security Decision Directive 145, creating a central apparatus for policy on computer and telecommunications security; the Reagan administration also tried to create a "sensitive but unclassified" category of information, but withdrew its plans in the face of congressional protests. In 1987, Congress passed the Computer Security Act, transferring these responsibilities to the National Bureau of Standards, with the NSA acting as technical adviser. In July 1990, President Bush signed an order disbanding the NSA's National Security Computer Center, so as to conform to the new law.

The changes in the international order may also bring changes for the NSA. As noted, the NSA does not discriminate between "friendly" and "unfriendly" states in its work. The demise of the Warsaw Pact, however, may mean a shift of resources away from the A Group, perhaps to the G Group, as the executive and Congress place new emphasis on such transnational concerns as terrorism, narcotics, and proliferation – all of which may be more daunting problems than were the various issues of the cold war.

Other Departments

Several other departments have certain intelligence responsibilities. The two most prominent are the Department of Energy and the Department of the Treasury. The Energy Department is represented on both the NFIB and NFIC by the assistant secretary for defense programs, who is also the senior intelligence officer in his department. Intelligence functions are handled by the deputy assistant secretary for security affairs and the director of the Office of International Security Affairs. With the State Department, the Energy Department is responsible for the overt collection of information on foreign energy matters. Most of this information is derived from employees making trip reports, but there is no specific internal collection branch. The Energy Department also produces and disseminates foreign intelligence within its area and contributes to collection and analysis where its special capabilities are required.

The Treasury Department is also represented on the NFIB and NFIC by the special assistant to the secretary (national security), who also heads the Office of Intelligence Support and acts as the liaison between Treasury and other intelligence community elements. The Office of Intelligence Support is not an analytical producer, but serves to keep other offices in the Treasury Department up to date on relevant information, including operation of the department's Watch Office. The Office of Intelligence Support has a staff of 18 (10 for the Watch) and a budget of approximately $900,000.

The Treasury Department is responsible for the overt collection of general financial and monetary information and participates with the State Department in the overt collection of general foreign economic information. It also produces and disseminates foreign intelligence relating to U.S. economic policy. The foreign collection activities of the department are carried out by financial attachés in U.S. embassies. E.O. 12333 also stipulates the Treasury Department's responsibilities, through the Secret Service, to protect the president, the Executive Office of the President, and others against surveillance equipment.

12

Oversight Bodies

Congressional Oversight

Congressional oversight of intelligence is handled primarily by the House and Senate Intelligence committees. Both committees resulted from the congressional investigations of intelligence in 1975–1976 when it was decided that, among other problems, congressional oversight had been lax.

The House Permanent Select Committee on Intelligence was created by House Resolution 658 (95th Congress) in 1977. In the 102nd Congress (1991–1992), it had 19 members (12 majority and 7 minority), excluding the House majority and minority leaders, who are ex officio members. There are three subcommittees – Legislation, Oversight and Evaluation, and Program and Budget Authorization.

The Senate Select Committee on Intelligence was created by Senate Resolution 400 (94th Congress) in 1976. In the 102nd Congress, the committee had 15 members (8 majority and 7 minority), excluding the ex officio majority and minority leaders. Unlike the House committee, the Senate committee is considered bipartisan – that is, its composition does not reflect the actual party division in the Senate. It currently has no subcommittees.

Both committees have exclusive legislative and oversight jurisdiction over the CIA and the DCI, including budget authorization. The Senate committee also considers the nominations of the DCI and the deputy DCI. Both committees share jurisdiction over other intelligence components with the committees on armed services (the DIA, the NSA, and other Defense intelligence components), the Judiciary (the FBI), and House Foreign Affairs and Senate Foreign Relations (INR). Each of these committees also has representatives on the intelligence committees, as do the appropriations committees. Since 1980 both committees were to have received prior notification of "any significant activity," including covert action. As the mining of Corinto harbor and Iran-contra showed, however, these provisions were not always obeyed by the executive. Under the terms of the 1991 agreement between the Bush administration and Congress, the major abuses discovered in Iran-contra (oral or ex post facto Findings and delayed notification to Congress) were clearly seen as going beyond permitted norms; "in a timely fashion" was taken to mean "in a few days" under most, but not all, circumstances. The 1991 bill also gave covert action a legal definition.

The creation of these committees raised two major concerns: their ability to safeguard classified material and their overseers' becoming too friendly with the intelligence community. Both committees have rules concerning the unauthorized disclosure of information by members or their staffs; their record to date, although not unblemished, is certainly much better than any of the intelligence agencies they oversee. (In 1987, Senator Patrick Leahy, vice chairman of the Senate Intelligence Committee, resigned after allowing a reporter to see an as yet unreleased, but not classified, draft report on Iran-contra.) Both committees also have limits on the time that a member may serve in order to ensure regular rotation.[156]

Although both committees have similar jurisdictions, they do not work in tandem and have followed different areas of interest. There have been recurrent suggestions, most recently by the Special Review Board in 1987, that there be a single Joint Committee on Intelligence, but neither house nor committee has shown much enthusiasm for a merger.

A major problem for the intelligence committees – indeed, for all congressional committees, but compounded in this case by security concerns – is access to necessary information. Executive branch reluctance to release such information is part of the ongoing struggle between the branches. The continual updating of the law on intelligence oversight reflects some of the state of play in the intelligence area. The committees are always careful to point out that they do not view their requirement for prior information as entitling them to approve certain activities. As Corinto and Iran-contra showed, however, Congress is not always able to judge whether it is receiving all the information it needs or to which it believes it is entitled. Much depends on the willingness of the executive branch to be forthcoming or to comply with oversight provisions, some of which have been the subject of interpretation even after their enactment.

Access to information raises a second problem for Congress: the willingness to accept information carries with it the potential for being co-opted – especially if there is an operational failure in the area of covert action.[157] Committees may refuse information, so as not to be co-opted, which was the congressional stance until 1976. Or they may accept the information, which may mean at least passive cooption in the decision. In either case, the committees face unpleasant alternatives should the operation become controversial or go wrong. They will then be asked by colleagues and constituents why they didn't know in advance. Or, if they did know, why they didn't do something to prevent it? Neither position is enviable.

Finally, there is the problem that service on the Intelligence committees does not present any of the usual benefits for members. There is no direct payoff for constituents in terms of "pork-barrel" projects; members can say little about what they are doing or what they have accomplished; and diligent service means time away from other areas where there are greater political benefits. This is not to suggest that there is no value to a job that is worth doing for its own sake or that members will not serve solely for that reason.[158] Yet, for all of the allure of access to intelligence secrets, service on the committees can be a burden.

Executive Oversight

President's Intelligence Oversight Board

The President's Intelligence Oversight Board (PIOB) was created by President Ford in 1976 to monitor intelligence activities, especially with regard to impropriety or illegality. Although originally attached to PFIAB, the PIOB continued to function after President Carter abolished PFIAB.

President Reagan reconfirmed the PIOB's role in E.O. 12334 (December 4, 1981), which remains in force. The PIOB is now part of the Executive Office of the President. It consists of three members, with the chairman appointed from PFIAB. The order specifies that members are to be appointed from outside the government.

In the case of illegal activities, board members are to inform the president; reports of illegal activities received by the board are forwarded to the attorney general. The board is also responsible for reviewing internal agency guidelines and the practices and procedures of the intelligence community inspectors general and general counsels. The board customarily meets with the president annually to present its report and may meet at other times as circumstances require. The PIOB meets six times a year, again with additional meetings as required.[159] In 1991 PIOB had a permanent staff of two (one counsel and one secretary) and a budget of $65,000 for operating expenses (excluding personnel).

Iran-contra focused renewed attention on what has been the major issue concerning PIOB – that is, its ability to discover improper or illegal activity and to act upon it. PIOB depends on people coming to it with information; it has no investigatory powers to subpoena or take sworn testimony. It can independently initiate reviews of situations that come to its attention, but its capabilities remain limited, as was revealed during Congress's investigation of Iran-contra.[160]

President's Foreign Intelligence Advisory Board

PFIAB is the successor to the President's Board of Consultants on Foreign Intelligence Activities appointed by President Eisenhower to review intelligence activities and performance.[161] The board was discontinued by President Kennedy upon his inauguration, but then revived under its present name after the Bay of Pigs debacle.[162] Then, as now, the board was composed of individuals outside the government, usually with experience in some aspects of national security or foreign policy (including, in some cases, technologies pertinent to intelligence). PFIAB continued to function in this manner until May 1977, when President Carter disbanded it on the grounds that such duties could be handled by the NSC, the intelligence agencies, and the congressional committees.[163] Critics charged at the time that the main motive behind Carter's move was the desire to do away with a group of advisers who were more conservative than was the administration itself. Others held that DCI Turner had been behind the move to gain greater operational latitude.

The absence of an outside body dedicated to the review of intelligence operations and products was a major criticism of the Carter administration's intelligence policies. President Reagan reconstituted the board by E.O. 12331 (October 20, 1981); this was superseded by E.O. 12537 (October 28, 1985), which reduced PFIAB to "not more than sixteen members." Some argued that the board, with 21 members, had become unwieldy, as well as too contentious and even "strife-ridden." At the time of this new executive order, President Reagan dismissed 11 of the 21 members.[164] In 1990, President Bush further reduced PFIAB, to six members, putting greater emphasis on members with first-hand intelligence experience.[165]

PFIAB continues to be responsible for reviewing all intelligence operations, activities, and management. It has no authority over the intelligence community, but acts in an advisory capacity, reporting to the president at least semi-annually. In 1991, the board had a staff of six and a budget of $338,000.

As with the PIOB, the size of PFIAB's staff raises some questions about its effectiveness. There have also been problems with the size of the board and its ability to focus its attention on issues that successive presidents have thought to be most worthwhile. Although PFIAB's purely advisory role inherently limits its influence on intelligence policy, it has been able to offer guidance, perhaps most dramatically in its sponsorship of the Team A–Team B exercise. Given its longevity (with two brief interruptions) and the interest of so many presidents in regulating it, PFIAB does seem to have found an important niche in helping oversee intelligence activities.

13

Observations

During 1990–1992, much of the discussion about the intelligence community in the wake of the collapse of Soviet power and the apparent end of the cold war has unfortunately centered on organization. Organization does matter, but only to a point. Too often, moving the boxes around on an organizational chart is an all too easy refuge from more fundamental problems and issues.

The key issue facing the intelligence community is not central authority versus autonomy, proximity to versus distance from policymakers, or diversity versus redundancy. The key issue is the ability of the community to deliver timely, digestible, and accurate analysis to policymakers and the priority among the myriad areas of interest and concern. Although bad organization can greatly impede such an effort, the reverse is not necessarily true; even the best organization cannot ensure "good" intelligence. Good intelligence analysis can only occur if there are analysts and collectors as well as managers and consumers who understand each other's needs and limits, who can communicate easily and with confidence, and who have a shared sense of trust. Such an arrangement sounds idyllic, but it does happen periodically, albeit not across the board and not consistently within any one area or issue.

Other than scientific research, intelligence analysis is probably one of the most purely intellectual activities pursued regularly by the government. It relies on the abilities to sift and weigh disparate and often incomplete information, to develop a "feel" for an issue that allows analyses – or hunches – to transcend available data, and to write clearly and succinctly for an always overworked audience. Because all of this is being done within a large bureaucracy, there is the usual overlay of hierarchies, forms, meetings, deadlines, schedules, et cetera. But analysis, when well done, is a task far removed from these more mundane requirements.

The major organizational issues that have been debated within the intelligence community will never be settled with finality. Indeed, it can be argued that this is a good sign, indicating an ongoing ability to be flexible and to adjust to ever-changing issues and demands. It can also be argued that if the more important substantive issue of "good" intelligence is being addressed successfully, then the organizational issues are of much less concern. If it can be demonstrated, however, that current organizations or procedures are impeding the production and dissemination of intelligence, then important work needs to be done – and promptly.

Notes

1. A major problem for anyone writing about U.S. intelligence agencies and activities is the plethora of books that have appeared since Congress's investigations in the mid-1970s. No researcher can hope to read all that is available; indeed, the intelligence library now replicates the classic intelligence problem of "chaff" versus "wheat." Researchers and readers need to be careful and selective. See Mark M. Lowenthal, "The Intelligence Library: Quantity versus Quality," *Intelligence and National Security* 2, no. 2 (April 1987). One useful recent reference work is Bruce Watson et al., eds, *United States Intelligence: An Encyclopedia* (New York: Garland Publishing, Inc., 1990).

2. Two biographies of Donovan (with overly sensational titles) are Anthony Cave Brown, *The Last Hero: Wild Bill Donovan* (New York: New York Times Books, 1982), and Richard Dunlop, *Donovan: America's Master Spy* (Chicago: Rand McNally, 1982). See also, the older Corey Ford book, *Donovan of OSS* (Boston: Little Brown and Co., 1970). Thomas F. Troy's *Donovan and the CIA* (Frederick, Md.: Aletheia Books, 1981) is less straightforward biography than a discussion of Donovan's role in shaping the organization of the Office of Strategic Services and later the CIA.

3. In intelligence parlance, this analytical error is called "mirror imaging"–that is, projecting your own behavior onto another nation or individual.

4. Wohlstetter's study of the intelligence aspects of Pearl

Harbor is a classic, analyzing several different levels of intelligence. See Roberta Wohlstetter, *Pearl Harbor: Warning and Decision* (Stanford, Calif.: Stanford University Press, 1962).

5. See, for example, the *General Strategy Review* presented by the British Chiefs of Staff at the Roosevelt-Churchill meeting in Argentia Bay in August 1941; it includes subversion and propaganda among the tools for defeating Germany. See also the commentary of the U.S. Joint Board, drafted a month later. The British paper is in the Public Record Office, COS (41) 505, CAB 80/30. The U.S. response is in the National Archives, JB no. 325 (Serial 729), Record Group 225.

6. This was not unique to intelligence. Much of the rationale, organization, and working methods of the JCS were meant to provide a U.S. parallel to the British Chiefs of Staff organization.

7. See Barry M. Katz, *Foreign Intelligence: Research and Analysis in the Office of Strategic Services, 1942-1945* (Cambridge, Mass.: Harvard University Press, 1989). Katz has written what he calls an "intellectual history" of R&A. Besides showing R&A's heavy dependence on academia and on recent left-wing emigrés to the United States, Katz concedes that R&A did not, "by any stretch of the imagination, [make] a decisive contribution to the war" (xi); and "there is precious little evidence that the reports, analyses, and forecasts churned out in the Branch figured decisively in the determination of military or diplomatic policy" (196).

8. Katz, *Foreign Intelligence*, is a recent exception to this historiography of the OSS. For the operational emphasis, see Ford, *Donovan of OSS*, and R. Harris Smith, *OSS* (Berkeley, Calif.: University of California Press, 1972).

9. Troy, *Donovan and the CIA*, 217–229.

10. Demetrios Caraley, *The Politics of Military Unification* (New York: Columbia University Press, 1966), 30, 38.

11. Senate Committee on Naval Affairs, *Unification of the War and Navy Departments and Post-war Organization for National Security: Report to Honorable James Forrestal, Secretary of the Navy* (79th Cong., 1st sess., 1945).

12. On the lack of any historical continuity between OSS and CIA analytical efforts, see Mark M. Lowenthal, "Searching for National Intelligence," in *Intelligence and National Security* 6, no. 4 (October 1991):736–749.

13. Senate Select Committee to Study Governmental Opera-

tions with Respect to Intelligence Activities [hereafter cited as the Church Committee], *Final Report*, Book IV: *Detailed Staff Reports on Foreign and Military Intelligence–History of the CIA*, by Anne Karalekas (94th Cong., 2nd sess., 1976) [hereafter cited as Karalekas, *History of the CIA*], 10. The Karalekas study remains the basic tool for any history of the CIA from 1947 to 1975.

14. Troy, *Donovan and the CIA*, 371.

15. Pertinent extracts from the congressional hearings, reports, and debates can be found in Grover S. Williams, *Legislative History of the Central Intelligence Agency as Documented in Published Congressional Sources* (Washington, D.C.: Library of Congress, Congressional Research Service, CRS Report 75-5A, January 8, 1975), 25–150A.

16. Troy, *Donovan and the CIA*, 385.

17. Ultimately, only the first three DCIs–Souers, Vandenberg, and Hillenkoetter–were active duty military officers. Three subsequent DCIs–Smith, Raborn, and Turner–were retired officers, Turner retiring after becoming DCI. On the other hand, seven deputy DCIs have been military officers.

18. The responsibility for the protection of sources and methods was included at the insistence of the military, which had continuing qualms about the new agency, especially over sharing intelligence with it. The military agreed to do so, but only if this responsibility for safeguarding intelligence was levied and made clear.

19. Clark Clifford, *Counsel to the President* (New York: Random House, 1991), 166–169. Clifford's memoir stresses the procedural nature of the creation of the CIA–that is, it was intended to improve coordination of intelligence, not generate new analysis.

20. Karalekas, *History of the CIA*, 385.

21. Some CIA veterans argue that the emphasis on the "operations/analysis" split within the agency has been exaggerated, particularly in the study done by Anne Karalekas for the Church Committee. Even if the Karalekas study did overemphasize the degree of this bifurcation, the fact that future DCIs Helms and Colby were seen as coming from the operations "side of the house," or that Robert Gates was the first DCI to come from the analytical "side," indicates that there has been some sense of "we versus they" within the two major components of the CIA. Indeed, Robert Gates's second nomination to be DCI was delayed because of concern about his possible early knowledge of the Iran-contra

affair, largely growing out of the July 1991 conviction of Alan Fiers, former head of the DDO's Central American task force, and the impending indictment of former DDO Clair George; there were reports of concern within the DDO about how Gates would reshape the CIA. See Michael Wines, "A Nomination Sets Off Battle on CIA Role," *New York Times*, July 14, 1991, p. 1.

22. *The Central Intelligence Agency and National Organization for Intelligence*, a report to the National Security Council, January 1, 1949, passim.

23. After his retirement, Allen Dulles wrote *The Craft of Intelligence* (New York: Harper and Row, 1963), which reveals his predilection for the operational aspects of intelligence – that is, spying. For broader analyses of Dulles's career, see Leonard Mosley, *Dulles* (London: Hodder and Stoughton, 1978), which deals with the three Dulles siblings – Allen, John Foster, and Eleanor; and Stephen E. Ambrose with Richard H. Immerman, *Ike's Spies: Eisenhower and the Intelligence Establishment* (Garden City, N.Y.: Doubleday and Company, Inc., 1981), 181 ff.

24. House Foreign Affairs Committee, *Soviet Policy and United States Response in the Third World* (97th Cong., 1st sess., 1981), 219–220. The Tibet operation differed somewhat from the others in that it had a more modest goal – harassing Chinese occupiers rather than working toward their removal from that country.

25. Victoria Price, *The DCI's Role in Producing Strategic Intelligence Estimates* (Newport, R.I.: Naval War College, 1980), 61–63.

26. In all fairness to intelligence producers, this desire for unanimity was not unique to them and is a classic problem for bureaucratic committees. Indeed, this concept of consensus, which often results in "lowest common denominator" agreements, was also a hallmark of the Joint Board and continues within the JCS. In each of these cases one of the primary motivations for such a method of operation would appear to be a willingness to jettison more widely divergent but perhaps honestly felt viewpoints in favor of presenting a united front before "outsiders," be they the NSC as a whole in the case of NIEs, or the secretary of defense in the case of the JCS. Such a method of operating can also corrupt the entire process if it leads participants to create extreme positions that they will later bargain away to preserve those points most important to them.

27. Commission on Organization of the Executive Branch of

the Government, *Intelligence Activities*, a report to Congress (June 1955), passim.

28. Although Soviet heavy bomber and ICBM forces were overestimated, Soviet intermediate and medium-range ballistic missiles were underestimated, as were the rationales behind Soviet force development. On the intelligence estimates involved, as well as other U.S. intelligence estimates of Soviet strategic forces, see Lawrence Freedman, *U.S. Intelligence and the Soviet Threat* (London: Macmillan Press, Ltd., 1977); and John Prados, *The Soviet Estimate* (New York: Dial Press, 1982), 67–126. The political aspects of the missile gap debate can be found in Roger Hilsman, *To Move a Nation* (Garden City, N.Y.: Doubleday and Company, Inc., 1967), 163–164; Arthur M. Schlesinger, Jr., *A Thousand Days* (Boston: Houghton Mifflin Co., 1965), 317, 498–500; and Theodore C. Sorensen, *Kennedy* (New York: Harper and Row, 1965), 610–613.

29. William Burrows, *Deep Black: Space Espionage and National Security* (New York: Random House, 1986), 102.

30. In that regard, in the new CIA headquarters then being completed in Langley, Virginia, Dulles had the following quote from the New Testament (John 8:32) inscribed, inappropriately, in the entry: "And ye shall know the truth, and the truth shall set ye free."

31. Dulles was not made the sole scapegoat for the Bay of Pigs; Richard Bissell, the deputy director for plans, resigned 10 months later. Kennedy also did not reappoint any of the JCS members when their current terms expired. Army Chief of Staff General George H. Decker and the chairman, General Lyman H. Lemnitzer, had both been appointed in the autumn of 1960; they were relieved on September 30 and October 1, 1962, respectively. Air Force Chief of Staff General Thomas D. White had been appointed in 1957, and Chief of Naval Operations Admiral Arleigh A. Burke had been appointed in 1955; they were relieved on June 30 and August 1, 1961, respectively. A sanitized version of the postoperation inquiry into the Bay of Pigs can be found in *Operation Zapata* (Frederick, Md.: Aletheia Books, 1981). See also Schlesinger, *A Thousand Days*, 233–297, and Sorensen, *Kennedy*, 294–309, for the view within the Kennedy administration. Peter Wyden, in *Bay of Pigs* (New York: Simon and Schuster, 1979), offers a critical view of the entire operation.

32. See Hilsman, *To Move a Nation*, 68–72, for his view on the reform of INR. Before coming to INR, Hilsman had given

some thought to the role of intelligence at the national level. See his *Strategic Intelligence and National Decisions* (Glencoe, Ill.: Free Press, 1956).

33. This emphasis in McCone's "orders" did not mean that the Kennedy administration was uninterested in the operational aspects of intelligence. Indeed, there was a great emphasis during those years on the concept of counterinsurgency, in many ways a predecessor of the Reagan Doctrine.

34. Price, *The DCI's Role in Producing Strategic Intelligence Estimates*, 65.

35. "Text of Senate Summary on Soviet Buildup in Cuba," *New York Times*, May 10, 1963, p. 2.

36. Helms's career is reviewed and assessed in Thomas Powers, *The Man Who Kept the Secrets: Richard Helms and the CIA* (New York: Alfred A. Knopf, 1979).

37. Price, *The DCI's Role in Producing Strategic Intelligence Estimates*, 66–67.

38. This was the famous debate over the NIE containing an assessment of the enemy's order of battle. The debate went on during 1967 and then became a major embarrassment after the Tet Offensive in 1968. The method by which an agreed estimate was reached raised serious questions about the effects of the war on the intelligence process, as well as questions about how the NIEs were coordinated. Much of the debate centered on charges made by former CIA analyst Sam Adams, who argued that his higher estimates of enemy strength were suppressed as part of a political conspiracy. For a recent refutation of Adams's charges, see James J. Wirtz, "Intelligence to Please? The Order of Battle Controversy during the Vietnam War," *Political Science Quarterly* 106, no. 2 (Summer 1991):239–263.

39. The White House, *Reorganization of the U.S. Intelligence Community: Announcement Outlining Management Steps for Improving the Effectiveness of the Intelligence Community*, November 5, 1971.

40. Karalekas, *History of the CIA*, 83.

41. Church Committee, *Final Report*, Book I: *Foreign and Military Intelligence*, 79–82.

42. Price, *The DCI's Role in Producing Strategic Intelligence Estimates*, 67–68. On Schlesinger's reforms, see also William Colby, *Honorable Men: My Life in the CIA* (New York: Simon and Schuster, 1978), 329–334.

43. Ibid., 351–353.

44. Price, *The DCI's Role in Producing Strategic Intelligence Estimates*, 68–69.

45. Seymour Hersh, "Huge CIA Operation Reported in U.S. against Anti-War Forces, Other Dissidents in Nixon Years," *New York Times*, December 22, 1974, p. 1.

46. On the "Family Jewels," see Colby, *Honorable Men*, 340–342. Colby also used this opportunity to dismiss James J. Angleton, longtime head of CIA's counterintelligence. Colby had been urging Angleton's dismissal when Schlesinger was DCI, finding Angleton's concerns over Soviet penetration of the CIA (the famous "mole" or "moles") byzantine, while effectively tying the agency in knots. By dismissing Angleton at this moment, Colby linked him with the revelations concerning illegal domestic operations, although this was not the case. The dismissal remains controversial. For Colby's view, see *Honorable Men*, 334, 363–365. A largely more sympathetic view of Angleton can be found in the somewhat overly dramatic David C. Martin, *Wilderness of Mirrors* (New York: Harper and Row, 1980). Tom Mangold, *Cold Warrior: James Jesus Angleton: The CIA's Master Spy Hunter* (New York: Simon and Schuster, 1991), and David Wise, *Molehunt: The Secret Search for Traitors That Shattered the CIA* (New York: Random House, 1992) both stress the disruptive if not destructive effects that Angleton had within the CIA.

47. The provisions of Hughes-Ryan were further limited by the fact that the DCI has at his disposal a contingency reserve fund "for objects of a confidential, extraordinary or emergency nature" that he can use at his own discretion by signing a voucher [CIA Act of 1949, 50 U.S.C.A. 403j (b)]. When this fund is exhausted, as was the case in 1975 when the United States was giving aid to the UNITA faction in Angola's civil war, Congress has been able to play a more direct role in covert action decisions. In the case of Angola, Congress placed specific limits on defense appropriations and on CIA contingency funds, which effectively curtailed the U.S. program once the previously appropriated contingency funds were exhausted.

48. Rockefeller Commission, *Report to the President by the Commission on CIA Activities within the United States* (June 1975), passim.

49. For some, part of this feeling also stemmed from Colby's dismissal of Angleton in 1974. Colby defends his policy in *Honorable Men*, 406–407.

50. For a detailed account of the inner workings of the Church Committee, including the rationale behind examining these subjects, see Loch Johnson, *A Season of Inquiry: The Senate Intelligence Investigation* (Lexington, Ky.: University of Kentucky Press, 1985). Johnson, a Church aide on the committee, portrays both Church and the committee in a positive light, but his book also details Church's shortcomings in directing the investigation.

51. Church Committee, *Alleged Assassination Plots Involving Foreign Leaders* (94th Cong., 1st sess., 1975), 4–7, 256. Knowledgeable CIA veterans maintain that, although the United States knew of the planned coup against Diem, arrangements had been made with him to allow him to leave Vietnam peacefully. Diem changed his mind during the coup, setting off the events that led to his death.

52. House Select Committee on Intelligence, *Recommendations of the Final Report* (94th Cong., 2nd sess., 1976).

53. "The CIA Report the President Doesn't Want You to Read," *Village Voice*, February 16, 1976, pp. 69–92. For a further assessment of intelligence performance in several of these instances (Tet, the Yom Kippur War, Cyprus), stressing the role played by the intelligence consumers (i.e., policymakers), see Mark M. Lowenthal, "The Burdensome Concept of Failure," in Alfred C. Maurer et al., eds., *Intelligence: Policy and Process* (Boulder, Colo.: Westview Press, 1985), 46–52.

54. Church Committee, *Final Report* (94th Cong., 2nd sess., 1976).

55. Schorr was forced to resign from CBS News because he initially let it appear that another reporter, Lesley Stahl, was the source of the report.

56. Church Committee, *Final Report*, Book I: *Foreign and Military Intelligence*, p. 76.

57. Ibid., 77–78.

58. An example of why intelligence analysts are reluctant to make drastic revisions in major estimates was the severe skepticism the CIA encountered in some circles in May 1976, when it nearly doubled estimates of the amount of Soviet GNP allocated to defense, raising the estimates of 6 to 8 percent to 11 to 13 percent. Besides raising methodological problems (such as calculating the Soviet GNP, or the validity of dollars-rubles comparisons), the revision raised questions about past estimates and thus about continuing estimation capabilities. It is easy to understand

the bureaucratic pressure against drastically revising estimates from year to year.

59. Senate Select Committee on Intelligence, *The National Intelligence Estimates A-B Team Episode Concerning Soviet Strategic Capability and Objectives* (95th Cong., 2nd sess., 1978).

60. For example, in his July 15, 1977 speech accepting the Democratic nomination, Carter listed several recent "serious mistake[s]" including "the embarrassment of the C.I.A. revelations," which he characterized as a departure from the "sound judgment and good common sense and the high moral character of the American people." Carter also said, "We CAN have an American government that does not oppress or spy on its own people" [emphasis in the original].

61. Senate Select Committee on Intelligence, *The Soviet Oil Situation: An Evaluation of CIA Analyses of Soviet Oil Production* (95th Cong., 2nd sess., 1978).

62. Turner first became concerned about the DDO in April 1977, when he discovered that some employees were engaging in illegal moonlighting activities with former employees Edwin Wilson and Frank Terpil in connection with Libya. Those dismissed for these activities were unrelated, however, to the October reduction. Turner asserts that only 17 people were fired and that 147 were forced into early retirement in October, but admits that these actions were not handled very "humanely." See Stansfield Turner, *Secrecy and Democracy: The CIA in Transition* (New York: Harper and Row, 1985), 55–59, 195–202.

63. Turner, *Secrecy and Democracy*, 5, 92–93, 206–207, argues in favor of new technical means, albeit somewhat defensively. He believes (p. 211) that the DDO resisted this emphasis out of their own sense of pride at being displaced and that this typified their refusal to be "a member of a team." His remarks also give some indication of Turner's view of the DDO in general.

64. Price, *The DCI's Role in Producing Strategic Intelligence Estimates*, 69–72.

65. Senate Select Committee on Intelligence, *Whether Disclosure of Funds Authorized for Intelligence Activities Is in the Public Interest* (95th Cong., 1st sess., 1977).

66. Senate Select Committee on Intelligence, *Annual Report to the Senate* (95th Cong., 1st sess., 1977).

67. An identical bill was introduced in the House as H.R. 11245, but it was the Senate committee draft. The House commit-

tee had not been in existence long enough to allow it sufficient time to participate significantly in the drafting.

68. House Permanent Select Committee on Intelligence, *Annual Report* (95th Cong., 1st sess., 1978), 6–9.

69. The note was actually instigated by the bureaucratically aggressive Brzezinski, who also worked to reduce Turner's access to President Carter. The fact that part of the handwritten note became public was indicative of the problem of leaks, which became a major focus of administration attention. Given the note's origin as a bureaucratic ploy, however, it is not surprising that it did become public. See Zbigniew Brzezinski, *Power and Principle: Memoirs of the National Security Adviser, 1977-1981* (New York: Farrar, Strauss, Giroux, 1983), 367; and Turner, *Secrecy and Democracy*, 113–114.

70. House Permanent Select Committee on Intelligence, *Iran: Evaluation of U.S. Intelligence Performance Prior to November 1978* (96th Cong., 1st sess., 1979).

71. On these problems, see, in addition to the House Intelligence Committee report cited above, Gary Sick, *All Fall Down* (New York: Viking Penguin, 1985), 90–92, 104–108, 193.

72. See, passim, Freedman, *U.S. Intelligence and the Soviet Threat*; Prados, *The Soviet Estimate*; and Burrows, *Deep Black*.

73. "Verification" refers to the process of making policy decisions about the intelligence received and assessed and the activities observed; it also covers decisions about the raising of these issues with the treaty partner, as well as policy responses to issues raised by the treaty partner. The actual gathering of intelligence, which goes on regularly whether or not there are arms control negotiations or agreements, is called "monitoring."

74. The major areas of Soviet violation claimed by critics at that time were the installation of a banned ABM radar in Kamchatka; the testing of surface-to-air radar in an ABM mode; the development, testing, or deployment of a mobile ABM; the construction of additional ICBM silos; the deployment of "heavy" ICBMs (SS-19); the inadequate dismantling of ICBM launchers replaced by submarine-launched missiles; the launching of additional missile-bearing submarines; the encoding of telemetry during flight tests; the concealing of certain activities; and the jamming of U.S. monitors.

The State Department responded to several of these in a report submitted to the Senate Foreign Relations Committee on

February 21, 1978. See Department of State, Selected Documents, no. 7.

75. See President Carter's January 17, 1979 press conference, *New York Times*, January 18, 1979, p. A18, and Department of Defense News Release No. 153-179, April 5, 1979.

76. In the jargon of arms control, the term "verifiability" is one that many practitioners eschew, as it cannot ultimately be determined. Instead, successive administrations have stressed the "adequacy" or "effectiveness" of verification for any provision or treaty.

77. Senate Select Committee on Intelligence, *Principal Findings on the Capabilities of the United States to Monitor the SALT II Treaty* (96th Cong., 1st sess., 1979).

78. Senate Foreign Relations Committee, *The SALT II Treaty* (report) (96th Cong., 1st sess., 1979), 189–228.

79. CIA's Directorate for Intelligence (DDI) had been redesignated NFAC in October 1977.

80. Only seven committees actually received briefings, as the House Armed Services Committee relinquished its role upon the creation of the House Intelligence Committee.

81. The bill also provided for prior notice of covert action to a more limited group, as well as a waiver of prior notice, which would then require a statement from the president explaining why prior notice had not been given.

82. House Foreign Affairs Committee, *The Role of Intelligence in the Foreign Policy Process* (96th Cong., 2nd sess., 1980), especially vii–xi.

83. For some examples of this problem, which affected many policy areas other than intelligence, see Frank J. Smist, Jr., *Congress Oversees the Intelligence Community, 1947–1989* (Knoxville, Tenn.: University Press, 1990), 124; and Turner, *Secrecy and Democracy*, 88.

84. One Carter administration decision that certainly alienated the intelligence community early on was the October 1977 indictment of former DCI Richard Helms for failing to testify "fully, completely and accurately" before the Senate Foreign Relations Committee in 1973 regarding operations in Chile. Helms pleaded "no contest" to the charge, stating that he had acted to protect certain information from unauthorized disclosure. The administration's decision to allow this plea to two misdemeanor charges also provoked criticism from those who felt it was too

lenient. Helms was fined $2,000 and given a suspended two-year prison sentence. Former CIA employees contributed money to pay the fine.

85. The 1980 Republican Party platform plank on intelligence can be found in Robert Ruhl Simmons, "Intelligence Policy and Performance in Reagan's First Term: A Good Record or Bad?" *International Journal of Intelligence and Counterintelligence* 4, no. 1 (Spring 1990):2.

86. Joseph Persico, *Casey: From the OSS to the CIA* (New York: Viking, 1990), is a sympathetic but not uncritical biography.

87. As they left the hearing room, a CIA staffer accompanying Casey was overheard saying: "Don't they [i.e., the senators] know who gets to make nominations?"

88. Senate Select Committee on Intelligence, *Report on the Casey Inquiry* (97th Cong., 1st sess., 1981).

89. That same day President Reagan also signed E.O. 12334, establishing new guidelines for the Intelligence Oversight Board.

90. In 1979 Deputy DCI Frank Carlucci, testifying before the House Intelligence Committee, said that FOIA requests cost the CIA $2.6 million and 116 staff years of work annually. The FBI put its FOIA-related costs for the period 1974–1979 at more than $29 million, entailing the allocation of 309 employees for 1979.

91. Joseph C. Goulden, *The Death Merchant* (New York: Simon and Schuster, 1984), relies heavily on interviews with former business associates of Wilson's; Peter Maas, *Manhunt* (New York: Random House, 1986), concentrates more on the effort to bring Wilson to justice and relies on the documentary record and interviews with assistant U.S. attorney E. Lawrence Barcella. On Terpil's subsequent activities, see Brian Duffy, "The Mystery Man in the Lockerbie Case," *U.S. News & World Report*, March 9, 1992, p. 44.

92. As noted above, this concept was not very far removed from the counterinsurgency concept in vogue during the Kennedy administration.

93. The text can be found in Theodore Draper, *A Very Thin Line* (New York: Hill and Wang, 1991), 20–21. Goldwater, who found the episode personally embarrassing, said succinctly: "I am pissed off!"

94. For more detail on this affair, see Simmons, "Intelligence Policy and Performance in Reagan's First Term," 15–17. Simmons

was the staff director of the Senate Intelligence Committee at the time and is credited with first discovering the truth about the Corinto operation.

95. For the text of the Casey accords (formally known as "Procedures Governing Reporting to the Senate Select Committee on Intelligence [SSCI] on Covert Action"), see Senate Select Committee on Intelligence, *Nomination of Robert M. Gates*, Senate Hearing 100-241 (100th Cong., 1st sess., February 17 and 18, 1987), 16–17.

Casey had also been hurt by reports in 1983 that he had made some large stock transactions, the second time his finances were at issue. In July 1983, Casey agreed to put his holdings in a blind trust. In 1985, Casey's taxes for 1976 became an issue, regarding the value of some patents for which Casey had taken a deduction. A federal tax court judge ruled Casey had overvalued the patents, which were valueless at the time.

96. As noted above, the DCI has at his disposal a contingency reserve fund against which he can draw simply by signing for it. These are authorized and appropriated funds and must be accounted for, but they give the DCI flexibility, especially for covert activities. Despite this unusual arrangement, all other rules for Findings, notifications, etc., still apply when using this fund.

97. A convenient guide to the often tangled history of Congress's action on the contras is Nina M. Serafino and Maureen Taft-Morales, *Contra Aid: Summary and Chronology of Major Congressional Action, 1981–1989* (Washington, D.C.: Congressional Research Service, Report no. 89-611, November 1, 1989).

98. See two articles by Stuart Taylor, Jr., in the *New York Times*: "Disclosing Secrets to the Press: U.S. Calls It Espionage," October 8, 1984, p. 13; and "Federal Judge Rules Espionage Laws Apply to Disclosure to Press," March 15, 1985, p. A15.

99. Pete Earley, *Family of Spies: Inside the John Walker Spy Ring* (New York: Bantam Books, 1988), gives an inside look into how the ring operated. Earley had extensive interviews with the three arrested Walkers, other family members, and Whitworth. Earley admits paying for the interviews, but notes that the various fines levied on the spies will probably preclude their receiving payment. John Barron, *Breaking the Ring* (Boston: Houghton Mifflin Company, 1987), tells the story from the viewpoint of the agents who broke the Walker case.

100. Howard maintained that he only passed this sort of information after his defection and not before, as was charged. David Wise, an author on intelligence issues who has often been critical of U.S. intelligence policies and practices, met with Howard in Budapest after his defection and concluded that Howard did provide the Soviets with information before his defection. See David Wise, *The Spy Who Got Away* (New York: Random House, 1988).

101. Wolf Blitzer, *Territory of Lies* (New York: Harper and Row, 1989), largely reports the Pollard affair from Pollard's point of view. Blitzer dismisses Pollard's rationale for providing the information to Israel, questions the degree to which this was an Israeli "rogue operation" versus a largely witting case of espionage against the United States, and concludes that the political repercussions for Israel far outweighed whatever information Pollard provided. Seymour M. Hersh, *The Samson Option* (New York: Random House, 1991), argues (285–286) that Pollard provided details on targets in the southern USSR for potential Israeli nuclear attacks.

102. On the Yurchenko affair, see Persico, *Casey*, 461–465, 467–470; Wise, *The Spy Who Got Away*, passim; Bob Woodward, *Veil: The Secret Wars of the CIA, 1981–1987* (New York: Simon and Schuster, 1987), 423–424; and Ronald Kessler, *Escape from the CIA* (New York: Pocket Books, 1991).

103. Senate Select Committee on Intelligence, *Meeting the Espionage Challenge: A Review of United States Counterintelligence and Security Programs* (99th Cong., 2nd sess., 1986); and House Permanent Select Committee on Intelligence, *United States Counterintelligence and Security Concerns—1986* (100th Cong., 1st sess., 1987).

104. Iran-contra has produced thousands of pages of documents, hearings, reports, testimony, etc. A useful one-volume synthesis of this wealth of material and of the various complex stories up to the November 1986 public revelations is Draper, *A Very Thin Line*. Draper says he has "let the facts speak for themselves." Although he does not achieve that level of objective detachment, Draper's book is an extremely useful, detailed account.

105. TOW stands for "tube-launched, optically-tracked, wire-guided."

106. President's Special Review Board, *Report of the President's Special Review Board*, February 26, 1987.

107. Even in death, Casey remained controversial. Much of the controversy stemmed from whatever role he played in Iran-contra and the uncertainties he left behind, but there were other incidents. At Casey's funeral, the presiding bishop used the eulogy to take issue with the policy of backing the contras. In the autumn of 1987, Bob Woodward published *Veil*, which detailed Casey's tenure as DCI, especially the operational aspects. *Veil* was based on extensive, but usually unattributed, interviews, including many with Casey himself. Much of the controversy surrounding *Veil* stemmed from two issues: Woodward's practice of attributing thoughts and direct quotes to individuals without giving the sources and Woodward's account of what he claimed was his final and climactic interview with Casey in the DCI's closely guarded Washington hospital room, which some doubted to have taken place.

108. Senate Select Committee on Secret Military Assistance to Iran and the Nicaraguan Opposition/House Select Committee to Investigate Covert Arms Transactions with Iran, *Report of the Congressional Committees Investigating the Iran-Contra Affair* (100th Cong., 1st sess., 1987).

109. This was especially apparent within the State Department, where analyses from INR that questioned contra capabilities ran afoul of the policy preferences of the Inter-American Affairs Bureau, headed by Elliott Abrams. Some INR analysts referred to this sometimes acrimonious debate as the "war with Elliott." See Frank McNeil, *War and Peace in Central America* (New York: Charles Scribner's Sons, 1988), 217–218, 241–247, 291–292. In October 1991, Abrams pleaded guilty to two misdemeanor counts of withholding information from Congress about secret efforts to aid the contras.

110. On July 28, 1987, Senator Leahy announced his resignation from the Senate Intelligence Committee, stating that he had violated committee rules when he allowed a reporter to see a draft report on Iran-contra. The report was not classified, but had not yet been released. This came at an especially embarrassing time for the committee, which had just promulgated its new rules for the handling of classified information. It also seemed to buttress the contentions of some, including Poindexter and North, that Congress could not be trusted to keep a secret – an allegation wholly unsupported by the weight of experience, given the far larger number of leaks that come from the executive.

111. Some members of the Intelligence Committee were particularly incensed by a December 17, 1986 legal opinion signed by Assistant Attorney General Charles Cooper, which held that the current obligation to provide "timely notice" left the president with wide discretion as to when that had to be done.

112. In June 1987, the Senate Intelligence Committee sent a letter to the new national security adviser, Frank Carlucci, a former deputy DCI, giving the committee's suggestions for new oversight requirements. As a result of these discussions, President Reagan issued National Security Decision Directive 286, which included key provisions that appeared later in the Senate bill, but did not meet the committee's requirements over the timeliness of notification to Congress. See Senate Select Committee on Intelligence, *Report Authorizing Appropriations for Fiscal Years 1990 and 1991* . . . , Senate Report 101-174 (101st Cong., 1st sess., 1989), 21–23.

113. See Ronald Kessler, *Moscow Station* (New York: Charles Scribner's Sons, 1989) for the details of the Marine case. Lonetree was sentenced to 25 years; Bracy, who recanted, later received an honorable discharge. A presidential commission headed by former Secretary of Defense Melvin Laird concluded that U.S. Ambassador Arthur Hartman was responsible for the lax security atmosphere in Moscow, a charge that Hartman refuted.

114. In 1987, the Senate Intelligence Committee issued a report, *Security at the United States Missions in Moscow and Other High Areas of Risk* (100th Cong., 1st sess., 1987), which called for the demolition of the new building in Moscow.

115. "Candor Is on Moscow's Wavelength," *New York Times*, December 14, 1991, p. 6.

116. In September 1989, the Soviets agreed to dismantle Krasnoyarsk. In an October 1989 speech before the Supreme Soviet, Foreign Minister Eduard Shevardnadze admitted that Krasnoyarsk was a violation.

117. House Permanent Select Committee on Intelligence, *Intelligence Support to Arms Control* (100th Cong., 1st sess., 1987), 27.

118. Senate Select Committee on Intelligence, *The INF Treaty: Monitoring and Verification Capabilities* (100th Cong., 2nd sess., 1988), 9.

119. The full text of President Bush's October 30, 1989 letter can be found in House of Representatives, *Conference Report:*

Intelligence Authorization Act for Fiscal Year 1991, House Report 101-928 (101st Cong., 2nd sess., 1989), 27.

120. The text of President Bush's November 30, 1990 Memorandum of Disapproval can be found in *Congressional Quarterly* 48, no. 49 (December 8, 1990):4119.

121. Covert action is defined in the new law (Title V of the National Security Act, Sec. 503 [e]; 50 U.S.C. 413) as

> an activity or activities of the United States Government to influence political, economic, or military conditions abroad, where it is intended that the role of the United States Government will not be apparent or acknowledged publicly, but does not include –
>
> (1) activities the primary purpose of which is to acquire intelligence, traditional counterintelligence activities, traditional activities to improve or maintain the operational security of United States Government programs, or administrative activities;
>
> (2) traditional diplomatic or military activities or routine support to such activities;
>
> (3) traditional law enforcement activities conducted by United States Government law enforcement agencies or routine support to such activities; or
>
> (4) activities to provide routine support to the overt activities (other than activities described in paragraph (1), (2), or (3) of other United States Government agencies abroad.

122. Senate Select Committee on Intelligence, *Authorizing Appropriations for Fiscal Year 1992 . . .*, Senate Report 102-117, (102nd Cong., 1st sess., July 24, 1991), 9. The committee actually proposed releasing three figures: the aggregate requested by the president; the aggregate authorized to be appropriated by the Congress; and the aggregate amount actually spent by the executive branch.

123. "Webster Admits CIA Flub on Iraq," *Washington Times*, May 14, 1991, p. 3.

124. In the post-World War II period, British intelligence, which had much better ties in the region, had been a major intelligence collector and producer in the Middle East. After Britain withdrew from "east of Suez," the United States was not able to fill the subsequent intelligence gaps.

125. Schwarzkopf's critique was part of his testimony before the Senate Armed Services Committee, June 12, 1991. See also,

Department of Defense, *Conduct of the Persian Gulf Conflict: An Interim Report to Congress* (July 1991), pp. 14-1–14-3.

126. See the Senate Intelligence Committee report cited in note 122, pp. 5–7.

127. "C.I.A.'s Track Record Stands Up to Scrutiny," letter by Richard J. Kerr [dated October 18, 1991], *New York Times*, October 24, 1991, p. A24.

128. It is not clear if this was done specifically to remove the DCI from this round of political changes, as had been the practice from 1953 to 1973, or was part of a larger pattern of retaining some senior officials from the Reagan administration. Besides DCI Webster, holdovers included Treasury Secretary Nicholas Brady, Attorney General Richard Thornburgh, and Secretary of Education Lauro Cavazos.

129. See Andrew Rosenthal, "White House Aims to Sharpen Role in Panama Plots," *New York Times*, October 13, 1989, p. A8; and Maureen Dowd, "2-Summit Plan Reflects Bush Style: Intense (Relaxed) Personal Diplomacy," *New York Times*, November 6, 1989, p. A14.

130. In November 1991, Duane R. Clarridge, a former senior DDO officer, was indicted on seven counts of perjury and making false statements in connection with Iran-contra. Clarridge, who had been removed as CIA's head of counterterrorism by DCI Webster after an internal review of Iran-contra, denied his guilt.

131. Michael Wines, "Intelligence Chief Tells about His Plan for Reorganizing," *New York Times*, December 5, 1991, p. A1.

132. Elaine Sciolino, "U.S. Reviews Focus of Security Data," *New York Times*, December 22, 1991, p. 9.

133. Robert M. Gates, *Statement on Change in CIA and the Intelligence Community*, April 1, 1992.

134. Gates testified that in 1980, which he described as "the high point of our commitment of resources to the Cold War," the Soviet Union absorbed 58 percent of intelligence resources, dropping to 50 percent by 1989. He said that in the budget submitted in 1992 the Commonwealth of Independent States would receive 34 percent of total intelligence resources. He subsequently said that 40 percent of new tasks would involve international economics.

135. Elaine Sciolino, "C.I.A. Panel Rejects View That Reports Were Slanted," *New York Times*, February 7, 1992, p. A13; and Elaine Sciolino, "C.I.A. Chief Is Upset over 'Politicization' Seen within Agency," *New York Times*, March 28, 1992, p. 1. The

issue was not yet behind Gates, however. On April 3, 1992, Gates took public exception to a *New York Times* editorial saying that he had "put the best spin" he could on intelligence regarding China and North Korea so as to buttress administration policies. See Robert M. Gates, "Keeping Politics and Intelligence Separate," Letter, *New York Times*, April 3, 1992, p. A24.

136. On this issue, see Mark M. Lowenthal, "Tribal Tongues: Intelligence Consumers, Intelligence Producers," *Washington Quarterly* 15, no. 1 (Winter 1992):157–168.

137. The DCI is sometimes referred to erroneously as director of the Central Intelligence Agency, a title that does not exist.

138. When the deputy DCI is chairing the NFIB, the "senior intelligence manager of the CIA," presumably the DDI, serves as the CIA representative.

139. Mark M. Lowenthal, *The National Security Council: Organizational History*, Report no. 78-104F (Washington, D.C.: Congressional Research Service, June 27, 1978), passim. See also, Joel M. Woldman, *U. S. Presidential National Security Advisers: Changing Roles and Relationships*, Report no. 87-334F (Washington, D.C.: Congressional Research Service, April 15, 1987).

140. E.O. 11905 abolished the NSC Intelligence Committee, USIB, IRAC, and the "40" Committee. This last body was replaced by the Operations Advisory Group.

141. President Reagan's six national security advisers were Richard Allen (1981–1982); William Clark (1982–1983); Robert McFarlane (1983–1985); Vice Admiral John Poindexter (1985–1986); Frank Carlucci (1986–1987); and General Colin Powell (1987–1989).

142. House Permanent Select Committee on Intelligence, *Annual Report* (96th Cong., 2nd sess., 1980), 12–13.

143. See above, note 125.

144. Admiral Bobby Inman, former deputy DCI and director of NSA and one of the few intelligence officers to achieve four-star rank, recently remarked that there are few career paths leading to flag rank for intelligence officers. See Senate Select Committee on Intelligence, *Review of Intelligence Organization* (102nd Cong., 1st sess., March 21, 1991), 25.

145. The 1986 Goldwater-Nichols Act put renewed emphasis on the importance of "jointness" within the military, giving this status as a career specialty, and requiring certain types of joint service before an officer could be considered for promotion to flag rank.

146. In 1973, the Senate Special Committee to Study Questions Relating to Secret and Confidential Government Documents inadvertently listed the National Reconnaissance Office in its report, although this did little more than acknowledge NRO's existence. See the committee's report, *Questions Related to Secret and Confidential Documents*, Senate Report 93-466 (93rd Cong., 1st sess., 1973), 16. See also, "Report 'Blows Cover' of Top Secret Agency," *Los Angeles Times*, December 25, 1973, p. 14.

147. Burrows, *Deep Black*, 135–136.

148. Ibid., 199; Philip Taubman, "Secrecy of U.S. Reconnaissance Office Is Challenged," *New York Times*, March 1, 1981, p. 12.

149. Taubman, "Secrecy," and Burrows, *Deep Black*, 201.

150. Webster's comments can be found in "New York City: Hotbed of Soviet Spies," *U.S. News & World Report*, January 18, 1982, pp. 30–31.

151. Sharon LaFraniere, "FBI to Seek More Funds to Fight Gang Violence," *Washington Post*, January 10, 1992, p. A3. A few months later, however, DCI Gates noted, "The KGB may have disappeared, but the interests of the Russian intelligence service in Western technology continues." He also said that the GRU – military intelligence – apparently had become more aggressive in technological espionage. See Bruce Van Voorst, "We See a World of More, Not Fewer, Mysteries," *Time*, April 20, 1992, p. 62.

152. This section deals only with the intelligence organization of the air force, army, and navy. Marine intelligence, although separate, is a much smaller unit than the others, with five main subsections: Counterintelligence/HUMINT, Intelligence Manpower/Training, Intelligence Plans and Estimates, Signal Intelligence and Electronic Warfare, and National Intelligence Affairs.

153. "Levels of confidence" is an intelligence term meaning the strength of conviction that an analyst has in his or her analysis, based on sources, analyses, professional expertise, and judgment. These levels are often expressed by such terms as "high," "moderate," or "low," but they are far from precise or stark gradations and are often akin to "gut feelings" about an issue.

154. See, for example, House Permanent Select Committee on Intelligence, *Iran: Evaluation of U.S. Intelligence Performance Prior to November 1978* (96th Cong., 1st sess., 1979), 4–8; and House Foreign Affairs Committee, *The Role of Intelligence in the Foreign Policy Process* (96th Cong., 2nd sess., 1980), x and 71–79, 131–137, passim.

155. James Bamford, *The Puzzle Palace* (Boston: Houghton Mifflin Co., 1982), 89–117.

156. House rules permit members to serve additional terms. For example, Rep. Dave McCurdy resigned from the House Intelligence Committee in 1987 after almost five of the allowed six years. McCurdy rejoined the committee in 1989 and became chairman in 1991, after incumbent chairman Rep. Anthony Beilenson reportedly was unable to persuade Speaker Tom Foley to change the service limit to eight years. Rep. Bill Young has also served more than one six-year term.

157. Although this apparently has not yet happened regarding covert action, the case of the War Powers Act in Beirut in 1983 is an instructive example. After President Reagan introduced marines into Lebanon in 1983, Congress insisted that he seek a War Powers Act authorization for them to remain there, the first time such an authorization was sought and voted. Not long after, a terrorist destroyed the Marine barracks, killing over 240 Marines. The fact that Congress had approved the deployment probably deflected much of the criticism Reagan would have received had there been no vote.

158. For a detailed discussion of the pros and cons of serving on the Intelligence committees from the point of view of members of Congress, see Smist, *Congress Oversees the United States Intelligence Community, 1947–1989*, pp. 89–93, 144–146, and 223–224.

159. These data are taken from the testimony of Bretton G. Sciaroni, who was counsel to the PIOB during the Iran-contra affair. See Joint Hearings before the Senate Select Committee on Secret Military Assistance to Iran and the Nicaraguan Opposition and the House Select Committee to Investigate Covert Arms Transactions with Iran, *Iran-Contra Investigation* (100th Cong., 1st sess., part 100-5, June 2–9, 1987), 393, 429.

160. In 1985, the PIOB investigated Iran-contra and concluded that the NSC was not covered by the Boland amendment. This investigation came in reaction to two events: (1) newspaper reports saying that Oliver North was giving military advice to the contras and (2) an inquiry to the NSC, also prompted by these reports, from Rep. Michael Barnes.

161. E.O. 10656, February 6, 1956.

162. E.O. 10938, May 4, 1961.

163. E.O. 11984, May 4, 1977.

164. Peter T. Kilborn, "Reagan Drops 11 in Foreign Policy Advisory Group," *New York Times*, November 5, 1985, p. A15. The new executive order also made a change in PFIAB's authority, changing the phrase: "3. The Board shall receive, consider, and *take* appropriate action . . . " to "3. The Board shall receive, consider, and *recommend* appropriate action . . . [emphasis added]."

165. Michael Wines, "Bush to Streamline Advisory Panel on Intelligence," *New York Times*, March 16, 1990, p. A9.

Index